GLOBETROTTER
ISLAND GUI

Madeira

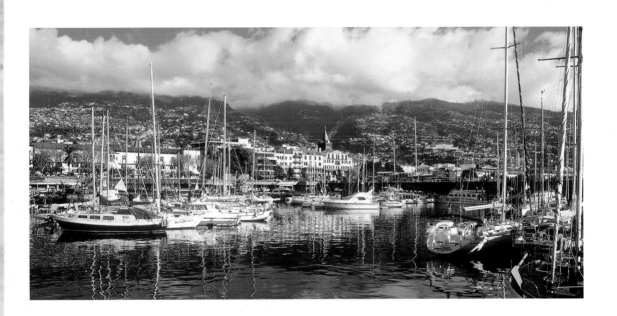

NEW HOLLAND

GLOBETROTTER™
ISLAND GUIDE
Madeira

Terry Marsh

Contents

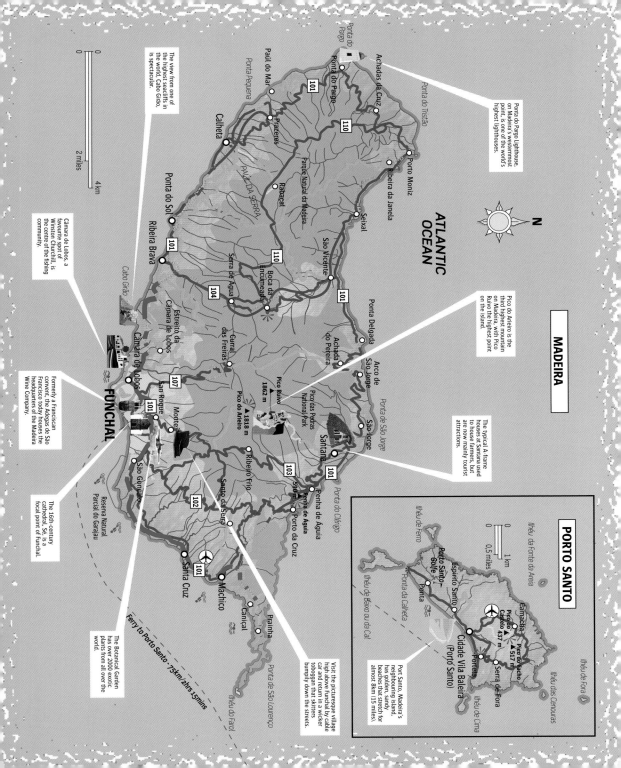

MADEIRA

ATLANTIC OCEAN

N

Scale: 0 — 2 miles, 0 — 4 km

Ponta do Pargo Lighthouse, on Madeira's westernmost point, is one of the world's highest lighthouses.

The view from one of the highest seacliffs in the world, Cabo Girão, is spectacular.

Câmara de Lobos, a favourite spot of Winston Churchill, is the centre of the fishing community.

Formerly a Franciscan convent, the Adegas de São Francisco today houses the headquarters of the Madeira Wine Company.

The 16th-century cathedral, Sé, is a focal point of Funchal.

The Botanical Garden has over 2000 exotic plants from all over the world.

Pico do Arieiro is the third highest mountain on Madeira, with Pico Ruivo the highest point on the island.

The typical A-frame houses at Santana used to house farmers, but are now mainly tourist attractions.

Visit the picturesque village high above Funchal by cable car and return in a wicker toboggan that skitters bumpily down the streets.

Ferry to Porto Santo · 75km/ahs 45mins

Place names (Madeira)
Porto do Pargo, Porta do Pargo, Achadas da Cruz, Porto Moniz, Ribeira da Janela, Seixal, São Vicente, Ponta Delgada, Arco de São Jorge, São Jorge, Ponta do Tristão, Paúl do Mar, Ponta Pequena, Prazeres, Rabaçal, Calheta, Ponta do Sol, Ribeira Brava, Serra de Água, Boca da Encumeada, Curral das Freiras, Achada do Teixeira, Pico das Pedras National Park, Santana, Penha de Águia, Porto da Cruz, Ponta de São Jorge, Ponta do Clérigo, Cabo Girão, Estreito da Câmara de Lobos, Câmara de Lobos, São Roque, Monte, FUNCHAL, Pico Ruivo 1862 m, Pico do Arieiro 1818 m, Ribeiro Frio, São Gonçalo, Santo da Serra, Reserva Natural Parcial do Garajau, Santa Cruz, Machico, Canical, Prainha, Ponta de São Lourenço, Ilhéu do Farol

Road numbers
101, 110, 104, 107, 102, 103, 59m

PARQUE NATURAL DA MADEIRA
PAUL DA SERRA

PORTO SANTO

Scale: 0 — 1 km, 0 — 0.5 miles

Port Santo, Madeira's neighbouring island, has golden, sandy beaches that stretch for almost 8km (15 miles).

Camacha, Pico do Castelo 437 m, Pico do Facho 517 m, Porto Santo Golfe, Espírito Santo, Cidade Vila Baleira (Porto Santo), Portela, Serra de Fora, Ponta

Ilhéu de Ferro, Ilhéu da Fonte da Areia, Ilhéu das Cenouras, Ilhéu de Cima, Ilhéu de Fora, Ilhéu de Baixo ou da Cal, Ponta da Calheta

Island Escape

Supervised by an old man leaning on a weighty stick, a haystack is working its way up the twisting road to Poiso. Beneath the huge mound of hay two feet appear, labouring slowly uphill. As I pass, I see that it's the man's wife carrying the load. No comment; except that such sights are not rare on Madeira; the old way of life still very much prevails, never far beneath the surface of everyday life.

Further on, beside the road, a farmer has parked his van and is selling flowers, strawberries, papayas, avocados and peaches from wicker baskets, while his wife offers bunches of scented camomile. At the other extreme, young people are having the time of their lives in the hotel pools and on the golden sandy beaches at Calheta, while parents and those who are here just to relax are sheltering beneath huge umbrellas, sipping Pimms, sangria or a Madeiran wine.

Madeira is like that; a place of gentle extremes that appeals to anyone. In recent times, the island has un-veiled a new tourist image, directing its marketing efforts towards a younger clientele, under the heading 'Body. Mind. Madeira'. The new concept is designed to appeal to the notion of self discovery in harmony with the nature of Madeira, capitalizing on the sense of well-being that the island arouses while simultaneously highlighting the numerous 'active tourism' assets like sport, water sports and walking, as well as health spas and wellness centres.

Described as a 'lush green speck' in the Atlantic, the island grows on you, very quickly. A balmy climate and seas warmed by the Gulf Stream, Madeira is a tropical island without the clamminess of the tropics; a place where the sun shines.

Madeira itself is an island of dazzling natural contrasts, too. From botanic gardens filled with a kaleidoscope of the world's richest trees and plants the landscape rises to barren volcanic peaks. And the World Heritage primeval laurissilva forests of the interior mark a different pace of life from the bustling, businesslike sophistication of the capital, Funchal. Nor could the difference be more noticeable than between the constant assault of Atlantic waves crashing around the island's shores and the hushed gurgling of water-filled channels (levadas) that ingeniously convey water around the island in one huge man-made irrigation system. Madeira is a part of Europe yet a part of something inestimably unique, somewhere else, further afield. Above all, Madeira is a place to unwind, recharge, invigorate and restore; a place for discerning travellers of all ages, young and old alike; a place for people with their finger on the pulse of all things refined and sophisticated, fun-filled and friendly.

Wholly committed to tourism – Madeira was one of the first major tourist destinations – the island people face up to the responsibilities with all the panache of a race proud of their heritage among the pioneers of world exploration, a people much given to passion for their country, yet with an eye to the opportunities of the wider world. The islands of Madeira are a destination possessed of all the intangible, half-formed intrinsic virtues of island life: a remoteness, an insularity, a mutually dependent life style and culture, an otherness, an island-ness, an away-from-it-all-ness.

The mild climate and relaxed pace of life gently pushes you into a lull of dreamy wistfulness. And yet, if you can stir yourself, this is an island just as much for the energetic, the walkers, the divers, the surf riders and the explorers. Of golden sandy beaches there are none, except that imported to Calheta from Morocco and the natural beach of Porto Santo, but with almost every major hotel providing extensive swimming and sunbathing areas, poolside bars, and attentive staff, the gap is more than adequately filled.

Madeira is very much a place where the body can unwind, and the mind relax, a place where the sea breezes are forever tangled in the trees, and the welcome of the island people beyond reproach.

Left: *The lack of golden sand beaches has resulted in most hotels, like the Quinta da Bela Vista, having extensive and well-equipped swimming pools and bars.*

Portrait of an Island Paradise

Left: The long sandy beach on Porto Santo, the product of a different geology than Madeira, is hugely popular during the summer months, but at other times you can virtually have the whole golden swathe to yourself.

Blessed with a favourable climate and surrounded by the warm seas of the Atlantic Ocean, Madeira seems to be in bloom whatever the time of year. It is, in essence, just one rather huge garden with a species list more appropriate to tropical rain forests. At every turn in the road – and there are hundreds, probably thousands, of those – flowers from many countries – Asia, Africa, Australasia and the Americas – put on an unforgettable and seemingly endless display. Throw in a stunning and convoluted landscape of wild mountains, deeply cleft valleys and dramatic sea cliffs, and the result is an island that is irresistibly beautiful whatever the season.

Left: Dragon tree and garden display in the beautiful setting of the Quinta Jardins do Lago, Funchal.

Introducing Madeira

Roughly on the same latitude as Bermuda, Madeira is a Portuguese island dependency. The historic capital and focal point of life on the island is Funchal, home to almost half the total population. Strongly Portuguese in character and architectural design, contemporary Funchal is a lively, buzzing town set on a delightful coast, and with enough in the way of museums, restaurants, shops, bars, parks, gardens and historic buildings to provide welcome diversion from days of lazing in the sun.

Around Machico, the island's first capital, eastern Madeira is quite built up, although the glorious, rocky peninsula of Ponta de São Lourenço, the most easterly point of Madeira, boasts the island's only natural sandy beach. In the west, by contrast, Ribeira Brava, backed by lush banana plantations, is the only place resembling a resort along the otherwise virgin western coast, although other locations are catching up, and a blossoming surf culture looks set to make rather more of Jardim do Mar and Paúl do Mar, as does the beach resort at Calheta, built around sand imported from Morocco.

The northwest of Madeira is splendidly wild and rugged with dramatic hillsides fashioned by waterfalls. Here the main centres are São Vicente, a pretty village with volcanic caves nearby, and Porto Moniz, which has inviting natural sea pools.

Accessible by motorway from Funchal, Santana in the northeast of the island is renowned for its iconic triangular houses and the tiny village of Porto da Cruz set beneath the towering cliffs of Eagle Rock up which the intrepid and energetic can wander. It is in the northeast that the mountains rise to their greatest height in Pico Ruivo and Pico Arieiro, offering stupendous views across the island.

Below: Ponta de São Lourenço is a long, sinuous finger of land reaching eastwards beyond Machico, one that offers a typical landscape of eroded volcanic cliffs that so characterize the Madeiran coastline. This is the place where Nature created a masterpiece, a combination of rocks and sea, breathtaking in the extreme.

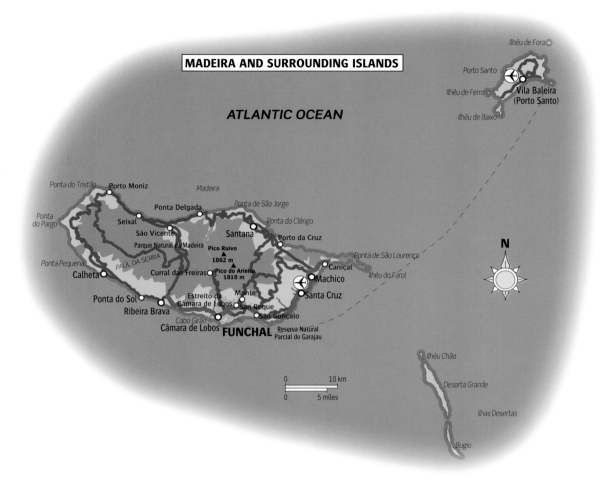

MADEIRA AND SURROUNDING ISLANDS

The Land

It is the sheer diversity of the landscape that is most astounding, cramming so much varied scenery into such a relatively small area. Beyond the towering, craggy, volcanic peaks, riven by dramatic gorges, the land is cloaked in primeval forest and fecund river valleys swathed in lush vegetation. And around the coast, instead of great arcs of sandy beaches, awesome cliffs dominate, rising near vertically in breathtaking fashion from very deep seas. Here, where the first settlers began cultivating the land, every square metre of usable land is turned to farming, often on perilously perched terraces (poios) which sag beneath the burgeoning weight of potatoes, corn, beans, vines and bananas.

Lying some 700km (440 miles) from the coast of Africa, and 1000km (600 miles) from continental Portugal to which it belongs, Madeira is not one island, but many. Collectively, the islands take their name from the largest, but in addition is made up of Porto Santo, some 50km (30 miles) to the northeast, and two groups of uninhabited islands: the Desertas and the Selvagens, roughly to the southeast.

The rugged, mountainous landscape of Madeira measures 796km² (307 sq miles) — 57km (35 miles) east to west, and 22km (14 miles) north to south; it contrasts remarkably with the island of Porto Santo, which is much smaller, having an area of only 42km² (16 sq miles) and, although anything but flat, having some rather shapely mountains of modest height, is quite arid. But what Porto Santo lacks in stature, it makes up for in a long swathe of excellent sandy beach, something which Madeira notably lacks. Christopher Columbus lived for a time in the island's capital, Cidade Vila Baleira.

To the southeast, on the horizon, lies a hazy group of islands; these are the Ilhas Desertas, meaning 'the deserted ones', or 'the Deserted Islands', so named because of the lack of permanent water and the barrenness of the soil. The whole group is a nature reserve, and rare species of bird and seal live and breed here. Much further afield lie the Selvagens, the 'Savage Islands'. This remote archipelago comprises two islands and several islets, all of them closer to the Canary Islands (165km; 100 miles) than they are to Madeira (280km; 175 miles), and represent the extreme south of Portugal. Officially the archipelago forms part of Madeira, but the Portuguese government has undertaken a study to set up a municipality (concelho) for the islands, which have only a single inhabitant, a guard.

Perhaps the most distinctive characteristic of Madeira is its system of water channels, or levadas. This ingenious network of open-air mini-canals was largely constructed by slave labour and conveys water around the island from the mountainous centre to the plantations lower down. The levadas, more than 200 in all, pass through spectacular scenery, and, dug by hand, stretch for more than 1500km (940 miles) linking remote villages through tunnels and along intimidating cliff-hugging ledges. 'Walking the Levadas' has become one of the major tourist attractions of Madeira, and is instrumental in bringing younger visitors to what had once unfairly been regarded as a destination for older generations.

Right: The north coast of the island, as here near Ponta Delgada, is superbly dramatic, and offers superb scenery that many consider is the finest on the island.

The Climate

Madeira's mild, subtropical climate played a huge part in attracting the first, mainly British, tourists at the beginning of the 19th century. With average temperatures of 24°C (75°F) in summer and 16°C (60°F) in winter, the climate of Madeira is very agreeable. Rainfall is rare in the warm season, especially on the south of the island, where it averages 550mm (22 inches) a year, but up to four times higher on the north side, which is more exposed to the wind. On a few days in the summer, when the 'Leste' blows — an east wind coming from the Sahara — temperatures can rise to a searing 40°C (104°F), and the air fills with fine Saharan dust.

Even so, most people living on Madeira consider that this is the most perfect climate in the world, overall neither too hot nor too cold. The Gulf Stream contributes to a sea temperature that is surprisingly warm. Moreover, the island has many microclimates which impact locally on weather patterns. The bay of Funchal, for example, protected by the highest peaks, enjoys the best of sunshine. Further down the west coast, at Ponta do Sol and Calheta, backed by the lower hills of the Paúl da Serra, the sun seems to shine brighter, but there is less protection from the sea winds. Often, too, the high ground may be shrouded in chilling mist that can linger through the morning, while the coast enjoys warm sunshine. The humidity around Funchal is rather more bearable, although the town is occasionally blanketed beneath cloud, the capacete, which clings to the town

MADEIRA	J	F	M	A	M	J	J	A	S	O	N	D
AVERAGE TEMP. °F	56	56	56	58	60	63	66	67	67	65	61	58
AVERAGE TEMP. °C	13	13	13	14	16	17	19	19	19	18	16	14
RAINFALL in	2.5	2.9	3.1	1.3	0.7	0.2	0.0	0.0	1.0	3.0	3.5	3.3
RAINFALL mm	64	76	79	33	18	5	0	0	25	76	89	84
Days of Rainfall	6.0	6.0	7.0	4.0	2.0	0.9	0.2	0.4	3.0	7.0	6.0	7.0

until mid-afternoon before retreating to the mountains. Thankfully, this phenomenon is not regular and tends to occur in the early part of the year, and in June, which locals call 'the month of the clouds'.

The prevailing wind is a northeasterly, gathering off the Portuguese coast and running down to the Cape Verde Islands. It brings moisture and large sea swells to the north coast, and often, particularly in the morning, adversely affects the weather on the eastern end of the island between Caniço and Caniçal. However, when a westerly blows, these areas can be surprisingly dry and sunny.

A Healthy Place To Be

Madeira has long been sought for the therapeutic qualities of its climate in curing respiratory illnesses, an attraction that continues to this day, and is still actively promoted under the modern banner of 'Wellness'. Most of the major hotels offer facilities to pamper body and soul, but some are real health resorts that combine medical and beauty treatments like thalassotherapy, hydromassage, Turkish baths, massages and beauty centres. You actually feel better just thinking about it!

Geography

Madeira is a volcanic island, although all volcanic activity ceased more than 400,000 years ago, when it put the finishing touches to the caves at São Vicente. Everywhere the telltale signatures of volcanic action remain, and are evident in the dark-coloured, mainly rocky, beaches and the widespread occurrence of basaltic lava pierced by dolerite dykes. Porto Santo is much the same, but is older than Madeira and has a central band of sandstone that has eroded to provide a long and splendid sandy beach less than a three-hour ferry ride from Madeira.

None of the text books or data sources agree, but somewhere between 2 and 20 million years ago the islands of Madeira were 'born' at the time of a series of cataclysmic submarine eruptions. Layers of rapidly cooling lava and igneous rock gradually built up from the seabed until a cone-shaped island finally rose above the surface of the ocean. But what does appear above sea level might be

***Below:** Panoramic view of the rugged and lush hinterland of the island, a place of vegetated mountainside and cultivation terraces from which the islanders eke a living.*

regarded as the tip of a lava 'iceberg', the rest of which, more than 3500m (11,500ft), is hidden underwater.

The main axis of Madeira, formed by those ancient volcanoes, lies east-west, in which line it follows a mountain chain, the backbone of the island, with a mean altitude of 1220m (4000ft) into which deep ravines penetrate from both coasts. The highest point of the island, accessible by a stupendous walk, is the Pico do Ruivo at 1862m (6108ft), significantly higher than anything in Britain, but rather less than the Alps or Pyrenees. More than 50% of the island lies above 700m (2295ft), and the cliffs at Cabo Girão, at 589m (1932ft) rank as the fourth highest sea cliffs in the world.

To the west of the highest summits, steep-sided ravines that rise to the mountain pass at Encumeada effectively split the island in half, north to south. West of this, more than 1400m (4593ft) above sea level, lies a wide, windswept moorland plateau, the Paúl da Serra, austere and yet endlessly fascinating. Towards the east, the landscape is marginally less dramatic, a place where the shapely peaks of the centre give way to a gentler flow of slopes and plateaux.

In the south of the island little remains of the laurissilva forest that once cloaked the entire island until the original settlers cleared the land, supposedly for farming, by setting it all ablaze – ironically, the name 'Madeira' means 'wood' in Portuguese. Even so, in the north some of the valleys still contain a fine spread of laurissilva forests (see page 20) and are now protected.

A long, narrow and comparatively low rocky promontory forms the eastern extremity of Madeira, and here there is a stretch of calcareous sand, known as the Fossil Bed, similar to that found on Porto Santo, and containing land shells and numerous shapes resembling tree roots of ancient origin.

A Natural Park For All

Conscious of the biological wealth of its natural ecosystems, in 1982 Madeira's regional government declared two-thirds of the island a nature reserve – the Parque Natural da Madeira. The protected area also includes the laurissilva forests, the Desertas and the Selvagens islands, the Natural Reserve of Garajau, and the Natural Reserve of Rocha do Navio.

The principal island of the Ilhas Desertas is Deserta Grande with a length of 12km (7 miles), then Ponta de São Lourenço, Chão ('flat'), the smallest and northernmost island, and Bugio ('monkey'). The islands are the last refuge of the monk seal, a status that led the Regional Government to designate the islands as a protected area, a condition that extends to a total ban on scuba diving in the reserve and a requirement that advance permission is needed before anyone can anchor near or visit the islands.

The Selvagen islands are formed into two groups, most notably among which are Selvagem Grande, Selvagem Pequena and Ilhéu de Fora; collectively they have been a nature reserve since 1971, one of the oldest in Portugal. The flora is especially attractive on Selvagem Pequena and Ilhéu de Fora, where grazing animals have never been introduced. More than 90 species of plant occur on these islands, of which 10 are endemic. Not surprisingly, perhaps, the islands are a favoured (and protected) nesting ground for sea birds.

The Parcial do Garajau Nature Reserve, created in 1986, lies off the south coast of Madeira; it is a marine park that includes a strip running from the high tide mark out into the sea to a depth of 50m (164ft). Fishing is strictly forbidden within the reserve which is renowned for a variety of coastal fish species as well as groups of Atlantic manta ray, which visit the island every year.

Under the administration of Santana, the Rocha do Navio Nature Reserve was the last to be created, in 1997. It was established as a response to local demand, and embraces a strip of sea, a small island and a potential habitat for 'sea wolf' (monk seal). Access by open boat is permitted, but underwater fishing and the use of nets is forbidden.

Right: Flanked by African lilies the road winds steadily and dramatically upwards through stunning scenery to the mountain pass of Boca da Encumeada.

Flora

'Macaronesia' is a modern invented name for several groups of islands among which the islands of Madeira are included. These islands have a unique biogeography, and are host to many distinct plant and animal communities. Because none of the Macaronesian islands was ever part of a continent, the native plants and animals arrived via long-distance dispersal. One notable characteristic is that they preserve the remains of a great forest dating back to the Tertiary Era (65 to 1.8 million years ago). This forest formerly covered vast regions of the European continent, but glaciation led to much of its destruction. Remarkably, and largely due to the influence of an oceanic climate, some species were able to survive among the Atlantic islands. And so it is that today Madeira is the only region in the world with samples of this ancient forest, well preserved and with species in large number.

The bulk of the laurissilva forest occupies a coastal strip from 300m to 1300m (984ft to 4265ft) above sea level, and plays a crucial role in soil preservation. Scientifically regarded as a living relic, almost all of the forest was in 1999 awarded the status of a UNESCO World Natural Heritage site. It is especially luxuriant around Rabaçal at the western edge of the Paúl da Serra, where the delights of the laurel groves, the ferns, waterfalls and deep gorges seem so far away from the abrupt headlands of the coast. Among the tree species there are fine specimens of bay tree (*Lauris azorica*), which is used in cooking, and a local form of mahogany (Vinhático). Less widespread on Madeira than on Porto

Santo is the dragon tree (*Dracaeana draco*) which has a red-coloured resin (the so-called 'dragon's blood') and clusters of spear-like leaves.

Not surprisingly, Madeira has been described as the 'floating garden of the Atlantic', a setting decked with shrubs and trees from tropical areas all over the world – jacaranda, Australian banksia, Mexican frangipani, araucaria pines from Brazil, cedars from the Atlas mountains, Japanese wisteria, and the Bolivian Tipuana tipu. Exotic

Left: Flowers abound across the width and breadth of Madeira, but are especially abundant in the gardens of the many hotels, like the Quinta de Bela Vista. Not surprisingly, Madeira is known as the 'Floating Garden of the Atlantic'.

species such as strelitzia, anthurium, proteas, amaryllis, cymbidium orchid and lady´s slipper orchids are among the thousands of flowers in bloom all year round. Nor is the magnificent display confined to botanical gardens or the rural quintas. Bougainvillea flourishes along the riversides, jasmine perfumes many private gardens, and even the roadsides are awash with jacaranda. Amateur botanists arriving on Madeira may be tempted never to leave; in fact, it is largely due to the efforts of keen British botanists, who made the most of the perfect climatic conditions and fertile volcanic soil, that Madeira flourishes as it does. At any moment in time, at least one of the 750-plus species of plant found on the islands is in flower. And of more than 200 species of flower endemic to Macronesia, no less than 80 are indigenous to Madeira; most grow at altitude, above 1000m (3280ft), and include the lovely Madeira violet, geranium, sow thistle and the striking yellow foxglove.

Fauna

Overall the good news is that there is nothing on Madeira that is likely to render you serious harm; no dangerous animals, no poisonous snakes. The only exception, the largest known type of wolf spider (*Geolycosa ingens*) lives on uninhabited Deserta Grande.

Because the Madeiran islands form the summit of a steep-sided underwater mountain, the considerable depths – from 2000m to 4000m (6562ft to 13,124ft) – are not an ideal habitat for the more common species of fish. Nevertheless, in these deep waters there are around 250 species of fish, many with bright colours and fascinating shapes, and all of them the target of local fishermen who optimistically cast their nets in the hope of catching fish en route to breeding grounds. Most of these are seldom seen (except in the fish market or on menus), but at surface level there are dolphin, whale and porpoise, shark, eel, ray and flying fish, and occasional green turtles. The evil-looking, but very tasty, espada preta (black scabbard fish) is unique to the waters around Madeira, and survives between 800m and 1600m (2624ft and 5250ft) down in the Atlantic depths.

Of the 200-plus species of bird found in the Madeiran archipelago, 42 species have been listed as breeding in the islands; these include the Madeira little shearwater, Manx shearwater, Cory's shearwater, Madeiran firecrest, long-toed pigeon, green canary and Atlantic herring gull. The distant Selvagens islands in particular are an important sanctuary for rare birds like the white-faced storm petrel and Bulwer's petrel. But Madeira is not on any principal migratory route, and only rarely finds vagrants blown onto its shores. For the rest of the time, however, birdwatchers will still find plenty of interest.

The Levadas

The rain in Spain, they say, falls mainly on the plain, but in Madeira it falls on the north of the island, and therein lies a problem. Most of the sunshine and the potentially fertile land lies in the south. The question was how to get the abundant water supply from the north, to the south. The solution, an ingenious network of mini-canals or water courses called levadas (from the Portuguese word 'levar', to carry). This incredible series of channels conveys rain and spring water directly to the fruit orchards, vineyards and sugar plantations. Today the levadas spread their watery tentacles across an almost unbelievable 2150km (1335 miles) of Madeiran countryside, fed by naturally occurring springs and man-made reservoirs.

Now, while still serving their original purpose, the levadas have acquired another use – highways for walking. Beside each levada is a service path (of sorts). Some

Left: The Levada do Norte is but one of hundreds of linking waterways that network the island, bringing water from the north to the drier farm terraces of the south.
Following page: The Wellness and Botanical Gardens in the grounds of the Quinta Splendida are symptomatic of the wider tourism theme that promotes Madeira as a destination where relaxation and luxurious well-being are paramount. It is impossible not to chill out in such an opulent setting.

of these are broad and well maintained, others are narrow and run above significant drops. But they are all capable of serving the needs of walkers, and 'Walking the Levadas' now forms an important part of the island economy (see pages 160–161).

Gardens

With such a lush diversity of plant life, it is not surprising that the Madeiran people are proud of their botanical heritage, and much of it is available for visitors to see in a number of well laid-out gardens and parks. This is the easy (and safest) way of seeing plants not only from Madeira, but often from further afield, too. Of course, a drive around the island at any time of year will reveal unimaginable 'free-range' displays of botanical beauty, and the local people are accustomed to bemused tourists wandering around with cameras – just don't stop on hairpin bends or where the roads are narrow!

In many ways, driving around the island and seeing the inordinate array of plants, trees and shrubs in a natural setting is unquestionably the best way. What is most striking about doing so is the overwhelming sense of how virile a place Madeira is; just about anything seems to thrive and proliferate here. A luxuriant green mantle rests across the landscape, with plants of unimaginable beauty sprouting from the most unlikely places. But there are times when you want to see things more closely and at a more leisurely pace. Then Madeira's botanic gardens come into their own.

Very much dedicated to the science and culture of endangered plant species, the Botanical Garden (Jardim Botânico, Caminho do Meio, Funchal: open daily from 09:00–18:00) has more than 2000 exotic plants from all over the world, and is a star attraction. The mansion within used to be a private estate (Quinta de Bom Successo) and is now the Natural History Museum. The Monte Palace Tropical Garden has around 100,000 species on display, including azaleas, heathers, ferns and trees, along with 60 of the 72 known species of cycad. There is also an area devoted to Madeiran flora,

which includes the laurissilva varieties endemic to the Macronesian islands (Caminho do Monte or Caminho das Babosas – entrance directly opposite the cable car: open Monday–Friday 09:00–17:00). While in this neck of the woods, the Jardins do Imperador adjoin the Quinta do Monte. This quinta was once the home of Emperor Charles I of Austria, who died here, and the gardens of that day have been restored (Caminho do Pico, Monte: open Monday–Saturday 09:00–17:30).

A number of smaller gardens facilitate a daily dose of flower spotting without detracting from the many other attractions of Madeira: Quinta das Cruzes Garden is in the park attached to the Quinta das Cruzes Museum and holds displays of endemic and exotic plants (Calçado do Pico, Funchal: open Tuesday–Sunday 10:00–12:30 and 14:00–18:00); Quinta Magnólia Garden has a variety of exotic plants in the gardens of the quinta (Rua Dr Pita da Silva, Funchal: open daily 08:00–21:00). The Palheiro Gardens within the Blandy Estate, has some intriguing displays of flowers amid its lawns and lakes very much in the 'English' style. It was the first owner, the Count of Carvahal, who allowed his love of English landscapes to influence his designs when the estate was first laid out in 1804. Bought by John Blandy, the wine merchant, in 1885, it has remained in the same family ever since, and has displays of flowers from the Far East, Australia and South Africa (Caminho da Quinta do Palheiro: open Monday–Friday 09:00–16:00).

Lovers of orchids will delight in the Quinta da Boa Vista Gardens which, in addition to its vast orchid collection, featuring cymbidiums, paphipedilums and lycastes, also has sections devoted to bromeliads from South America, aloes from Africa and martinets from Australia (Rua Lombo da Boa Vista, Funchal: open Monday–Saturday 09:00–17:30, except public holidays). Owned by an Austrian in love with both orchids and Madeira, the Jardim Orquidea (Orchid Garden) displays a collection of over 6000 orchids, some of which are available for sale in sterile 'in vitro' jars, for safe transit home (Rua Pita da Silva, 37, Funchal: open daily 09:00–18:00).

Funchal

By no means central to the island, the Madeiran capital is superbly set on a natural sweeping bay above which a soaring backdrop of richly vegetated slopes rises to a skyline of rugged peaks. Setting aside the practical issues of landing and developing a new community here, the first sight of what was to become Funchal must have stirred the hearts of the pioneer settlers.

The name, Funchal, derives from funcho, the Portuguese word for fennel, large quantities of the aromatic plant being found along the banks of the rivers that here reach the sea. Half of Madeira's population today live in and around Funchal, so it is not surprising that it is better geared up to accommodate the tourist trade, encouraging most visitors to stay at least for a few days before moving on. But the island is so compact that were it not for the vagaries of Madeira's road network, many visitors would be tempted to stay in Funchal and travel out to the various corners on a daily basis. Thankfully, the spaghetti-on-a-plate design of the road system, entirely dictated by the landscapes of the island, encourages visitors to spend time further afield, and rightly so, for the island has much to offer the curious traveller.

To fully appreciate the magnificent setting of Funchal you need to take the Monte cable car and look back across the great sweep of the bay, while at the same time marvelling at how so many houses, hotels, apartments, offices and restaurants can be crammed onto a vast sloping hillside without somehow pushing one another down into the sea.

What an aerial view enables you to pick out are three distinct zones: the harbour area and the 'seafront', the western end where most of the hotels are found, and the Zone Velha (the Old Town), most easily pinpointed by the bright yellow buildings of the Forte de São Tiago.

Right: A network of streets spreads out from the centre of Funchal into the suburbs, inviting exploration. Most spring from the area around the cathedral and are a delight to walk. But, be warned: the further you walk from the centre, the steeper they become.

Above: If Funchal has a focal point, then it's around the 16th-century cathedral and the main square, the Praça do Municipio, the finest square in Madeira, beautifully and skillfully inlaid with recurring tile patterns that are said to represent fish scales. There is always activity here, people milling about, taxis and buses coming and going, cafés doing a brisk trade.

Moreover, as most of the key sights for tourists are within a couple of blocks of narrow streets from the harbour, the heart of Funchal can easily be explored on foot, and this is by far the best way.

If there is a focal point, then it's around the 16th-century cathedral (Sé) and the main square, the Praça do Municipio. There is always activity here, people milling about, taxis and buses coming and going, cafés doing a brisk trade, and a small number of people begging for money, though this aspect of life on Madeira is much less a problem than of old. Between the two, and along the main streets, is where you find the principal fashion and souvenir shops, although the bustling atmosphere of the famous covered market (Mercado dos Lavradores) and the adjacent gory fish market is a little further to the east. On the odd-shaped Largo do Gil Eanes, north of the cathedral, flower women shelter beneath awnings and behind a bright spread of orchids, protea and strelitzia. They invariably wear the traditional dress – striped skirt, white blouse and a waistcoat – although sadly this had almost fallen from everyday use until the tourist authority contrived a revival a few years ago, and now it is commonplace to see groups of flower sellers, dancers and singers in costume throughout Funchal.

The Hotel Zone to the west has its own assortment of bars and restaurants, and the island's casino, but the true atmosphere of Funchal seeps from the walls of the Old Town (the Zone Velha), where you can dine at a different restaurant every night, enjoying the Madeiran specialities, and listen to the style of singing known as fado, something akin to the blues. Here the cobbled streets, a web of small and narrow streets, are a maze in themselves and a delight to wander. The tiny houses are painted with bright colours, and many have been converted into bars and restaurants. Some of the oldest streets in Madeira are found here, many dating from the very early 16th century.

Funchal is a satisfying blend of old and new architecture; the design of the cathedral and the casino, for example, could hardly be more contrasting. Yet it all works well, the one age serving to complement the other. Museums (*see* Island Culture) and churches abound, historic buildings, parks and gardens, and a flotilla of catamarans, yachts and sailing boats all eager to carry you out to sea in search of turtles, dolphins and whales.

A good place to start is the Story Centre (*see* page 81) on the edge of the Old Town, that sets the scene and illustrates the essence of Madeira. From there, it is only a few strides to leap into the Monte cable car to be whisked to the eponymous mountain village from where a daring return to Funchal can be made aboard one of the unique wicker toboggans (carro de cesto) that skitters bumpily down the streets in hair-raising but enjoyable fashion.

But before you put your life in the hands of the very able men who 'steer' the toboggans, it is well worth investigating Monte itself. This remote hillside village was fashionable towards the end of the 19th century, when the nearby Palace Hotel ran a sanatorium for people with tuberculosis. The Monte Palace is now a

private home, but the surrounding gardens (*see* page 23) are a horticultural theme park with grottoes, fountains, ornamental bridges, Japanese structures, waterfalls, ponds, levadas and statues.

Close by is the Quinta do Monte, one of the finest rural hotels on the island (with an outstanding chef – *see* page 109), and directly above the start of the toboggan run, perhaps ominously, is the twin-towered Church of Our Lady of Monte, a distinctive landmark from many parts of Funchal especially at night when the towers are illuminated. The building dates from the early 19th century, but a chapel is said to have been built on this site by the first Madeirans born on the island (Adam and Eve apparently). On 15 August each year (the Feast of the Assumption), a medieval statue of the Virgin is the focus of worship for many islanders who climb the 74 steps leading to the church on their hands and knees as a mark of devotion. In the grounds of the church is a small marble chapel, the last resting place of the former emperor of Austria, Karl von Habsburg (*see* panel, page 70).

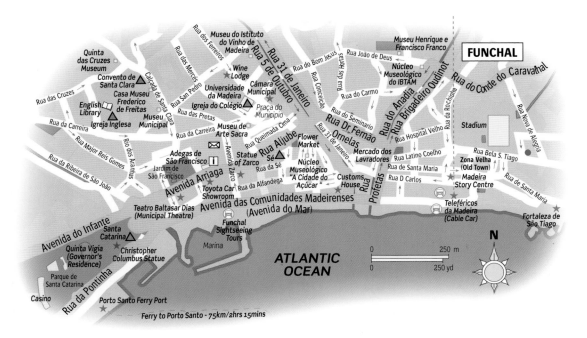

The Old Town: Cobbled Streets and Alleyways

First impressions can be misleading, and that gained of the Old Town, especially if you begin down the Rua de Santa Maria, the oldest street in Funchal, is no exception. Here on sharp-cobbled streets you encounter a run of seedy bars, but there is no danger to passers-by, and before long the bars give way to a welter of cafés and restaurants serving some of the tastiest food in Madeira, if not always in the most salubrious surroundings. Money was poured into the Old Town during the 1990s, and renovations galore have raised it from a period of crumbling neglect into a touristy, up-market, trendy zone that is constantly abuzz. Wander at will here, but be cautiously discerning about where you eat. At the far end, you reach the Fortaleza de São Tiago, begun in 1614, and extended in the 18th century. You enter the fort through an archway, and a ticket office just inside suggests that payment is necessary. But it isn't. The fort houses a contemporary art museum, and that's what the charge is for; you can wander freely around the fort itself, exploring arched passageways, facing the sea breeze on the fort ramparts. Along the narrow, missable Travessa do Forte canaries in cages still hang from windows, washing is strung across the street, and the elderly women of the Old Town sit gossiping on their doorsteps, or peering at you from shady doorways.

Mainstream Funchal

Back in Funchal there are a few key sights that figure on the tourist trail: the Convento de Santa Clara, for example, which once housed the oldest religious order on the island, founded in 1496. The first abbess, Dona Isabel, was the sister of João Gonçalves de Câmara, grandson of Zarco. Only the most affluent families sent their daughters (not always willingly) to Santa Clara, an enclosed order, where a commitment was for life. Today's few remaining sisters are Franciscans, and not so restricted. Sadly, the convent is a gloomy experience unless you are desperately keen to look at rooms full of motley religious iconography – reliquaries, altars, poly-

Above: *The Convento de Santa Clara once housed the oldest religious order on the island and here a commitment was for life, although today the few remaining sisters, all Franciscans, are less restricted.*

Right: *Azulejos are a beautiful and artistic way of portraying island life, and are found extensively in Funchal and in the many island villages. These decorated tiles are each a part of a larger piece of ceramic art on local themes.*

Previous page: *A view of Funchal Bay from the mountainous road to Poiso and Ribeira Frio; terracotta-roofed houses cling to the hillsides and seem in permanent danger of sliding into the sea.*

chrome statues and portraits of saints – that has seen better days. The adjoining church, however, is quite splendid if zealously over-ornate. Though nothing remains of his 15th-century chapel, Zarco is buried here, ignominiously under a wooden trapdoor in front of the high altar with its ornate silver sepulchre.

Just a few strides from the convent is the Quinta das Cruzes (see page 85), an archetypal Madeiran manor house erected on the site of a house said to have been built by Zarco. South of the convent, along the Calçada de Santa Clara, is the Casa Museu Frederico de Freitas (see page 88), a stunning town house and former home of Frederico Cunha de Freitas, a lawyer with a monumental appetite for collecting, amassing in his lifetime a priceless hoard of antiques, curios and objets d'art, including a bizarre assembly of over 2000 milk jugs, teapots and vases. A new wing to the museum contains a fine display of azulejos, the hand-painted tiles for which Portugal and Madeira are renowned.

Avenida Arriaga

The place that most attracts visitors, apparently, is the Adegas de São Francisco on Avenida Arriaga, today the headquarters of the Madeira Wine Company (see page 81), which may have something to do with its popularity. The buildings formerly belonged to a Franciscan convent, and date from the 17th century; in the 1840s they

Azulejos

Found throughout Portugal and across the island of Madeira, azulejos are painted ceramic tiles, first introduced into Spain by the Arabs during the Moorish occupation. Increasingly, they were used in Islamic architecture for facing walls and paving floors. During the 15th and 16th centuries, Portugal imported tiles from Spain for use in religious and private buildings, and they in turn exported them in the 17th century to the Azores, Madeira, and Brazil.

were acquired by the Blandy family which began producing wine on Madeira in 1811.

The Avenida Arriaga, partially pedestrianized, is the main drag from the hotel zone into town, its pavements with decorative mosaic patterns (calçateros) made from tiny blocks of white limestone and grey basalt which are then skilfully formed into geometric patterns, a skill that is still dominant on Madeira. At its western end the Avenida runs into the Avenida do Infante, which itself is bounded on the south by the refreshingly lovely Parque de Santa Catarina, a place for romantic people, flower lovers, joggers, yoga practitioners and those up early enough to catch the sunrise across the bay. In the grounds of the park, a sculpture of the 'Sower' (by Francisco Franco) is a reminder of the island's dependency on home-grown produce, while an east-facing statue of Christopher Columbus is a link with the past. Further west a large mansion overlooks a swan-filled lake: Quinta Vigia is today the official residence of the Madeiran president. You may get into the gardens on weekdays (if there are no functions), but don't expect an invite for a cup of tea.

Back on the Avenida Arriaga, almost opposite the Wine Museum, is the Toyota Car Showroom, unremarkable in itself, except for the splendid display of azulejos that could well earn this particular car showroom the accolade of the most attractive in the world. Close by, the local theatre is a significant venue for cultural events including recitals of classical music and, by contrast, a folk festival in October. The theatre café is also an excellent spot to stop off for a morning coffee, and, if your Portuguese is up to it, eavesdrop on the local gossip. Where the Avenida Arriaga meets the Avenida Zarco there stands, somewhat predictably, a huge statue of Zarco himself, once surrounded by traffic, but now sitting in the middle of the pedestrian zone.

Funchal's cathedral, Sé, dates from 1514, during the reign of Manuel I, and is an early example of Manueline architecture, something of a comfortable blend of Gothic and Renaissance styles. The architect, Pêr Annes, came from Alentejo in Portugal, and the Moorish influences that prevailed there have translated into his work in Madeira, most strikingly in the azujelo tiling of the roof. Surprisingly, given the elaborate work of the interior, the exterior façade is almost simplicity itself with its distinctive Manueline doorway above which is the king's coat of arms. Inside is another matter: the ceiling, in particular, is among the finest in Portugal, carved from native cedar trees and overlaid with ivory in Arabic designs. The choir stalls are by Flemish craftsmen, and, if you look closely, you'll see they offer amusing observations on life in Madeira in the 17th century in a manner not dissimilar to those found in French and English churches.

Beyond a rash of smart fashion shops on the Rua dos Ferreiros, lies the Praça do Municipio, the finest square in Madeira, beautifully and skilfully inlaid with recurring tile patterns that are said to represent fish scales. On its south side is the Museum of Sacred Art (see page 83), while to the north is the Church of St John the Evangelist (Igreja do Colégio); it is open only for services, but its exterior boasts some fine saintly statues. The adjacent buildings house the University of Madeira.

Anyone keen to pursue the history of wine making should visit the Rua dos Ferreiros where you'll find Artur de Barros e Sousa Lda. (ABSL), founded in 1921. Owned by Artur and Edmundo Olim, fourth generation descendants of the company's founder, ABSL is the smallest of the Madeira wine producing companies on the island. The current annual production of wine is only 8–10,000 litres. As with most producers, the Olim brothers don't own vineyards, but buy grapes from farmers around Jardim da Serra (Sercial), Campanario (Malvasia and Boal) and São Vicente (Verdelho).

The lodge that houses the company is a delight to visit, and has changed little in its 80 years. The smell of the old casks is overwhelming. Their most important market

Right: The buildings of the Adegas de São Francisco on Avenida Arriaga formerly belonged to a Franciscan convent, and date from the 17th century; in the 1840s they were acquired by the Blandy family who began producing wine on Madeira in 1811.

is Funchal, mainly selling their wine to people who enter the lodge. None of the wines undergo estufalgem (*see* page 145). In fact ABSL takes pride in being the only company to mature all their wines naturally by the traditional canteiro method, in tiered attics, rather than in warmed concrete vats.

No-one visiting Funchal should leave without dropping in to the covered market, the Mercado dos Lavradores. It's at the edge of the Old Town, though not part of it, being built quite recently, in the 1940s. It has some splendid azujelo decoration, and is set on two levels. This is the place to soak up the atmosphere of Funchal; the best time to visit being Friday and Saturday when

farmers from rural Madeira come into town with their rickety trucks full of flowers and vegetables. The flower sellers usually turn out in their colourful traditional costumes of striped skirts and red waistcoats, and the whole scene is a profoundly stimulating confusion of bartering, banter, chit-chat, gossip and bonhomie. Immediately adjoining is the fish market, where the catches come in, especially tuna and evil-eyed scabbard fish; it's not a place for anyone who can't stand the sight of blood.

And when you've had your fill of the market, chill out at one of the cafés nearby or in the Old Town in readiness for lunch.

Above: The entire coastline of Madeira is rugged beautiful
and no more so than along the north coast where tiny
settlements have carved a presence at the water's edge,
invariably backed by soaring vegetated cliffs.

Around the Coast

The coastal landscapes of Madeira, especially to the west of Funchal and along the north coast, are less well known than any other part. One reason is that until comparatively recently the 'west' really was 'wild', and difficult to access. In fact, at one time what is today's surfing centre, Paúl do Mar, was accessible only by boat. Things improved significantly in 1997, when the expressway (the ViaLitoral) opened, and today, heading west, you can pursue a tortuous, but hugely delightful route all the way to Porto Moniz – fascinating for car passengers but quite an ordeal for the driver!

The numerous tour buses that leave Funchal after breakfast head first for Câmara de Lobos, where Winston Churchill painted harbour scenes, then grind upwards to create traffic jams at the top of Cabo Girão, the fourth highest sea cliff in Europe, although other estimates suggest (erroneously) that it is the highest, or the second highest.

Beyond Cabo Girão, the coast runs on to Ribeira Brava where tour buses unload their clients for tea and a brief stroll before either heading back to Funchal, or north over the Boca da Encumeada (1007m; 3304ft) to São Vicente. Very few ever continue west, and yet along this neglected stretch of coastline lie some of the island's most agreeable villages, with good swimming and surfing. True, it has been, and remains, difficult to access. But road improvements have brought places like Calheta, Jardim do Mar and Paúl do Mar within easy reach of Funchal, although there is much to be said for making one of these resorts your base, and treating Funchal as a day trip destination.

At the furthest point, after a convoluted journey, possibly with a minor deviation to the westernmost point of the island at Ponta da Fargo lighthouse, you reach Porto Moniz, which is really quite special, and deserves to be on everyone's itinerary. Here the landscapes are steep, wild and rugged, nature in the raw, and all the more interesting for that.

The quickest way today to explore the southwest coast is to use the expressway (via rápida), but traditionally the route lay out of Funchal past Reid's Hotel, the first

major road to be built on Madeira. It was started in 1815, but proved very costly and soon ran out of money. By the 1850s it extended only a couple of miles from Funchal, and was used by tourists for short afternoon excursions. The expressway is undoubtedly much speedier, but the old road has the tang of nostalgia and an attractive alternative if you are not going far. It was along the coast here, at Praia Formosa, that Bertrand de Montluc landed in 1566 with 1000 French freebooters before striking for Funchal. Today, Praia Formosa, in spite of its black, bouldery beach and an unsightly oil refinery, is popular for swimming and supported by a few bars and food kiosks.

Câmara de Lobos

A short distance beyond Praia Formosa, lies the fishing village of Câmara de Lobos – the 'Chamber of the Wolves' – so called by Zarco when he discovered the bay in which monk seals were gambolling in the waves (a seal in Portuguese is called a 'sea wolf'). Alas, there are no monk seals here now; they are a protected species, and found only in the remote waters of the Ilhas Desertas. In 1420, Zarco built his first settlement at Câmara de Lobos, but it was not long before the more favourable anchorage at Funchal drew them away.

Today, the 'Chamber of the Wolves' is best known for its connection to Winston Churchill, who painted a number of harbour scenes here, and is openly marketed as such. It is certainly a very atmospheric, if shambolic spot, and the centre of the village, in spite of growing development around its edges, is an agreeable mish-mash of whitewashed houses, shops and bars. The beach, as with most Madeiran beaches, is black and rocky and doubles as the village harbour mantled by the smell of paint, tar and freshly sawn timber. Usually it is filled with colourful boats – small canoes for inshore fishing, and embarcações for deeper waters – in various states of repair,

Left: Named Cabo Girão ('turning point' or 'about turn' in Portuguese) because it was here in his exploration that Zarco turned back towards what was to become Funchal, this great craggy upthrust is the fourth highest sea cliff in Europe.

while the dock and bars are often filled with local men playing cards or dominoes. The tiny fisherman's chapel, Nossa Senhora da Conceição, said to be the second oldest on the island, has some naïve paintings of fishermen, shipwrecks and the life of St Nicholas, and merely serves to underline the dependency this village has on the sea, and the sorrow such reliance has brought.

Rue São João de Deus is a lively street filled with shops and bars, at the top of which you find the Igreja de São Sebastião, some of which dates from the 15th century, although most of it is 250 years younger; it houses some attractive azulejos.

The village of Câmara de Lobos is split in two by a rocky bluff. To the west of this, the Largo da Républica provides a lovely view of the nearby cliffs of Cabo Girão (early morning light is best). Here, too, is the sea-facing Rua Nova da Praia, above a modern promenade which winds around the rocky bluff back to the harbour.

Aesthetically, things have gone a little downhill since Churchill's day; or maybe he just used an artist's eye – you may well have to do the same if you are to overlook the evident poverty and industry. The life of a fisherman is neither easy nor wealthy.

Cabo Girão

For the record, Cape Enniberg in the Faroe Islands (750m/2460ft above the North Sea) is the highest sea cliff in Europe; then Preikestolen in Norway (604m/1981ft above Lysefjorden), Slieve League in Ireland (601m/1971ft above the Atlantic), and then Cabo Girão (589m/1932ft). But who's counting?

Named Girão ('turning point' or 'about turn' in Portuguese) because it was here in his exploration that Zarco turned back towards what was to become Funchal. There is a small viewing area at the top of the cliffs, thankfully adequately protected, from which you can look down on the tiny farmers' fields at the foot of the cliff – most easily accessed by boat – but you need a good head for heights. When the coach parties are not crowding the streets, this is a truly tranquil spot perfumed by aromas from the nearby pine and eucalyptus trees. But when the coaches arrive so too do the pan pipe players and the trinket traders. Make an early start and get up here before them; the way is signed from the expressway, from which you climb through plantations and terraces.

Ribeira Brava

If you arrive in summer, you might be forgiven for thinking that the translation of Ribeira Brava as 'wild river' is a mistake; the insipid trickle choked with grass and weeds can't possibly be the torrent that gouged a way through the impressively steep cliffs inland. But come in winter, when the mountains are being deluged, and you'll see a quite different beast, and one worthy of its name.

Surrounded by banana plantations, the small town of Ribeira Brava, a comfortable 30 minutes' drive from Funchal, is surprisingly energetic, a bustling place with ongoing work to build a new harbour that may one day replace the old one beyond the tunnel at the eastern end of the seafront. This is one of the oldest towns on the island, and was well established as a sugar producing area by as early as 1440 in the island's history.

If you want an easy day, this is the place to come, to take a coffee and chill out. The church of São Bento (St Benedict), founded in the 15th century, is the main attraction, possessing a lovely Baroque bell tower with clock and a chequerboard steeple that is really quite appealing. But there is a good range of shops that sell much more than the conventional tourist tat, specializing as they do in wickerwork, embroidery, glassware, etc. At the northern end of town, a pink, 16th-century town house accommodates the Museu Etnográfico da Madeira (Ethnographic Museum), which has displays on fishing, agriculture, winemaking and weaving, and it has a pleasant café.

The tourist office is housed in a miniscule tower that once formed part of a defensive system against pirates, and along the seafront a modest swimming area, ideal for families, sits above a small sheltered area of natural coastline. On the Feast of St Peter (29 June) paper flowers are strewn across the narrow, cobbled streets, and visitors arrive by boat to have barbecues of espetada on the stony beach.

Calheta

Anyone looking for golden sandy beaches must come to Calheta; even though the beach is imported, the sand is real. The long seafront forms a link between the new part of town, evolving around the beach area and marina, and the old town.

Calheta was given its town charter as long ago as 1502, and for many years was governed by Zarco's children. When sugar was a vital commodity, Calheta served as a customs post. Today, life in Calheta is much more relaxed, and the marina is an important base for water sports as well as boating and yachting.

***Below:** The Ponta do Pargo lighthouse, situated on Madeira's westernmost point, is one of the highest in the world.*

Above: Porto Moniz is a gem of a place, clinging to
the coast at the foot of stupendous cliffs cut by
cultivation terraces where farming goes on in
the old way, as it has done for ever.

Ponta do Pargo

The lighthouse below the village of Ponta do Pargo
marks the westernmost point of Madeira. The village is
surrounded by vineyards and fields of vegetables
worked, invariably, by tough-looking women. Here it is
still possible to see the land being farmed in the traditional manner, and detect something of the harmony
between Man and Nature.

The whole area around the lighthouse is an Important
Bird Area, a priority area for the conservation of
threatened or range-restricted birds. In the cliffs below

the lighthouse two rare seabirds are known to breed –
Cory's shearwater and the Madeira storm petrel,
while inland you might well spot linnets, buzzards,
Berthelot's pipit and spectacled warbler. A nearby tea
house makes the experience all the more engaging and
worth the short detour.

Porto Moniz

What brings people to Porto Moniz, other than curiosity,
is the system of seawater pools created by the reefs in
the lava rocks, which offer a chance to swim in the sea
without the pounding that the northern coastline seas
would otherwise generate.

The northwestern tip of the island is about as far from
Funchal as you can get, and there is ample justification
in that alone for spending a night or two here. Even if

you don't stay overnight, you need to plan to spend a whole day in getting to and from Porto Moniz. Perhaps the best way is along the north coast road from São Vicente or Santana. Much of this has been improved, and there are many tunnels, but, travelling east to west, it is still possible to use sections of the old, and rather scary, road. The route around the western coast, from Ribeira Brava and Calheta is about as tormented a road as you could hope to find, making ingenious use of contours, but sometimes ignoring them altogether. On a clear day, it is a splendid drive from Ribeira Brava up to the Boca da Encumeada. There turn left to cross the Paúl da Serra, near the highest point of which you have the choice of a right turn down to Ribeira da Janela, following a newly surfaced road, or of continuing to pass the Jungle Rain Café and hotel. You continue above the stunning gorges of Rabaçal, eventually meeting the west coast road a few miles west of Porto Moniz, which is then approached down a long and winding road with stunning views of the town and its new helipad way down below.

This is a gem of a place, clinging to the coast at the foot of stupendous cliffs cut by cultivation terraces where farming goes on in the old way, as it has done for ever. That visitors find this an attractive place is evidenced by a growth of new hotels, shops, banks, restaurants, a swimming pool and an aquarium. Swimming is safe in summer, but very often dangerous during the winter months.

Originally, the town was known as Ponta do Tristão, after the nearby headland, which marked the boundary between the two regions controlled by Captain Zarco and Tristão Vaz Teixeira during the 15th century. In 1533, however, management of the town fell to Francisco Moniz, who had the whit to marry Zarco's granddaughter, and so, in 1577, the town was named after

Left: The tiny smuggling village of Porto da Cruz clings to the black coastline of the northeast, but has seen a growth in popularity in recent years, with a large swimming pool and a rash of restaurants and bars.

him. Although the pounding waves may cause you to think otherwise, the harbour is quite sheltered, protected to a fair degree by the Ilhéu Mole. This quality brought Porto Moniz the wealth and distinction of becoming a major whaling centre, when whaling ships from the Azores began operations.

Today, Porto Moniz is a significant wine growing and fishing region with an important cattle fair that usually takes place during the summer months. But until tourism began having an impact towards the end of the 20th century, this was a remote and self-sufficient community, its people having to rely on what could be produced on its cultivation terraces and from the sea. The terraced fields above the old town are bordered by drystone walls, or fences made from bracken or broom, which provide shelter for the crops from the northerly winds.

The 'new town' stretches along the coast between the sea pools. The easterly pools are just below the aquarium, which is housed in an old fort, and are a series of rocky channels – not always filled with water – but which provide warm plunge pools.

The North Coast Road

Taken in its entirety from Porto Moniz to Santana, the road along the north coast is simply stunning. Motorists will be thankful that the old road, which can still be seen clinging desperately to the edges of the island in a few places (and still motorable if travelling from east to west), has almost now been replaced – there is still one narrow section near Ponta Delgada. But it provides superb coastal scenery that many say is the finest on the island.

The villages are generally small, but not without interest. Seixal makes its living from grape production, sercial being grown here and used to give the driest of the Madeiran wines. This is a peaceful hamlet and its fertile surroundings also favour mangoes, avocados, figs and apples. Otherwise there is little but calm to detain the tourist; swimming is tricky as the currents are strong along this stretch of coast. São Vicente has a little more

Above: Penha de Águia (Eagle Rock) lies on the eastern seaboard of Madeira, near Porto da Cruz, although there are no eagles there these days, and scant evidence that eagles were ever on the island.

about it. Made a municipality in 1743, the village nestles at the northern end of a steep-sided valley, and is really quite graceful. There are restaurants, bars, cafés and shops facing out to the sea, and a new bridge spanning the river sits either side of a tiny chapel, the Capela de San Roque, built in 1694 on the spot where St Vincent is supposed to have made an appearance. The main part of the village is a short distance inland, past some rather curious boulders balanced on poles. Around the church, dedicated to St Vincent and with the obligatory Baroque interior decoration and lavish gold leaf, cafés and bars cluster around in a gentle setting of cobbled streets and alleyways. Given the straightforward

and well-maintained access south through the mountains to Ribeira Brava, this would make an ideal alternative location for a few days while you explore the north coast and the Paúl da Serra. The main hotel is a short distance to the east (*see* page 116).

Not far from São Vicente a cave system (Grutas de São Vicente) was discovered by an Englishman in 1855. The caves are believed to have been formed 400,000 years ago, at a time when the volcanoes of the Paúl da Serra were active. As cave systems go, these are not very extensive, only 700m (2300ft), with just a mere 70m (230ft) open to the public.

Heading east, the road bypasses Ponta Delgada before making a significant detour inland to Boaventura and Arco de São Jorge. The countryside is lush and bright with flowers throughout the year, including some that grow only along the north-facing coastline. This, too, is where the willow is produced that is used in the wickerwork industry, along with increasing investment in grape production.

The enchantment of Santana, apart from its splendid restaurant (O Colmo), is the distinctive A-shaped houses, palheiros, which are found mainly in this part of the island. Triangular in shape, with steep gables, thatched roofs and just two tiny rooms, these traditional houses are increasingly falling into disrepair and being converted to use as farm outbuildings for storage or shelter for cattle. In past times, the upper storey would have been used for storing grain and other crops. Palheiros apart, Santana is, on the face of it, of limited appeal. But, just 20 minutes from the airport, it makes an eminently suitable alternative to a stay in Funchal. This is the starting point for a number of good walks through the

Pico das Pedras National Park to the Government-owned rest house at Casa das Queimadas. From here, where there is a place to have a picnic in the shade of the trees, there is a waymarked track through broadleaved woodland of beech and oak to Pico das Pedras, although there is an alternative, but more difficult route, along the Levada do Caldeirão, through lush virgin laurel forest and across two major ravines (torches are needed if anyone is tackling this walk, plus considerable experience, as the path is eroded in places).

At the entrance to Santana is the Madeira Theme Park (Parque Temático da Madeira), essentially an exhibition site devoted to the Madeiran way of life, with displays on wine making, sugar production, folklore and tourism; in the grounds you'll find ox carts, fishing paraphernalia, a windmill, a maze, boating lake and a replica of the train that used to run up to Monte above Funchal.

A short way inland from Santana, the village of Ilha, and, more to the point, the new road that now leads to it, takes you back in time. This is a highly rural part of the island, where the agrarian lifestyle of the Madeiran people is eked out. If you want to see how the traditional rural way of life goes on, this is a place to visit, but don't expect a rash of modern tourist facilities. From the village, and simply not shown on any maps, a farming service road takes a serpentine tour of the valleys and eventually emerges at São Jorge. It's a hairy experience, especially if you meet a tractor coming the other way, but if you can persuade a local taxi driver to take you

Left: The distinctive A-shaped, thatch-roofed houses are a big part of Santana's charm. Although farmers used to live in the houses, they are now mostly either tourist attractions or are being converted to use as farm outbuildings.

Following page: Said to be the place where man first landed on Madeira, Machico is just twenty minutes' drive along the expressway from Funchal and lies in a wide natural bay, backed by steep terraced slopes.

MACHICO

round it, you'll be treated to a picture of a way of life far removed from the trappings of modern tourism.

If you can't get anyone who admits to knowing the road, then you can get a good idea of the landscape from the miradouro at São Roque do Faial. It is a breathtaking sight, as is the immense rock itself, the Penha de Águia (Eagle Rock, although there are no eagles there these days).

On the far side of the rocks, the tiny village of Porto da

Henry Veitch

Henry Veitch was born in Selkirk, Scotland, in 1782, and came to Madeira early in the 19th century.

He was Consul General on the island from 1809 to 1836 and as well as having political interests, he was a successful wine merchant, and architect of the Madeira Wine Museum. He was also instrumental in building the English church and graveyard in Funchal. Of rather less acclaim, Henry Veitch is known to have had quite a number of mistresses, all openly 'installed' in his various residences, and his descendants on the island are said to be legion.

Cruz boasts a small black-sand beach, and has seen something of a growth in popularity as a seaside resort, with a large swimming pool and a rash of restaurants and bars. It really is quite unexpected.

Machico

Bright and bustling Machico is said to be the place where man first landed on Madeira. The man in question was Captain João Gonçalves Zarco, but, so legend has it, he came across the graves of two castaways, Robert Machim, an Englishman, and his mistress, Anna d'Arfet, and named the settlement he founded in their memory. As ever, a fine line divides legend from fact.

Writing in his diary following a visit to Madeira in 1837, one young Victorian traveller (Edward Watkinson Wells) said 'Machico is the oldest and most miserable place in Madeira.' Clearly, he was not impressed, but today's visitors will find quite a change. From a historic point of view this is probably the most interesting town on the island, boasting the oldest church, the Capela dos Milagres, and two forts that bear witness to defence against pirate attacks on the village.

Machico is just twenty minutes' drive along the expressway from Funchal and lies in a lovely natural bay, flanked by steep terraced slopes. The beach, although composed mainly of black rocks, does reveal a strand of dark sand at low tide, and this alone, with the excellent facilities in the town for lunch, makes Machico an ideal place, away from the bustle of Funchal. Little more than an overgrown village, Machico has a relaxing air and some better-than-average restaurants and cafés serving Madeiran cuisine with Spanish and Italian influences.

A focal point of Machico is the cobbled main square, Largo do Municipio, where taxi drivers waiting fares chat beneath aged oak trees. Close by is the 15th-century church, Igreja da Nossa Senhora da Conceição, thought to have been designed by Pero Anes, who also designed Funchal cathedral. The church is noted for its attractive south door which has three white marble pillars that were a gift from King Manuel I (1495–1521), who also donated the statue of Our Lady on the high altar, a poly-

Above: *The sea stacks along Ponta de São Lourenço would once have been linked to the island, but were isolated when the connecting bridge collapsed thousands of years ago. One day the stacks, too, will crumble beneath the waves.*

chrome carving of the 'Virgin and Child' (now held in the Museum of Sacred Arts in Funchal), and the organ. The church is believed to have been built at the instigation of Branca Teixeira, wife of Tristão Vaz, one of the first governors of Madeira, and, judging by the generosity of the king, she must have been a greatly favoured lady at the Portuguese Court. Although simple in design, the south door and its pillars is the finest Gothic arched doorway anywhere on the island.

Across the square the town hall is by comparison a youthful structure, dating from the 1920s, beyond which a humped bridge spans the course of the Ribeira Machico and the road leads to the tiny Capela dos Milagres (the Chapel of the Miracles) built in 1815 and thought to be on the site of an earlier chapel, the Capela do Cristo, where Anna d'Arfet (and possibly Robert Machim) were buried. Between the two chapels, there have been others invariably destroyed by floods. In 1803 the entire church was washed out to sea, but a wooden crucifix from the church was picked up by a passing gal-ley, an event the people of Machico regarded as a mir-acle, one that is commemorated each year on 8 October by a torchlit procession through the town. The chapel was damaged twice more by floods, in 1883 and 1957, and rather points to some alternative site – one less prone to flooding – being more suitable.

From the main town square, narrow streets lead down to the bay, passing the old market, now restored as a restaurant (Mercado Velho), with lovely jacaranda trees and a marble fountain. Directly opposite is the Forte do Nossa Senhora do Amparo, an unusual triangular fortress built in 1706, one of three originally built as defence against pirates. Another, Forte São João Baptista, near the quay, is now in private hands, while the third, on the western edge of the bay, was long since destroyed.

The sea front is modern, with 'New Age' buildings, and increasingly popular with tourists and locals seeking some time in the sun. The Machico Forum, a new cultural centre, sits both on the site of the town's football pitch and an underground car park.

Machico is a special place for Madeirans; of great historic significance, and today an appealing alternative base from which more widespread exploration is made possible by the expressway.

Ponta de São Lourenço

Ponta de São Lourenço, a long, sinuous finger of land reaching eastwards beyond Machico offers a landscape of eroded volcanic cliffs that so characterizes the Madeiran coastline. Without question, this is the place where Nature created a masterpiece, a fantastic combination of rocks and sea. It is a nature reserve, because of its flora.

If a complete tour of the island is beyond question, then a visit to Machico and out past Caniçal to this promontory will be rewarded with truly breathtaking scenery. Walkers should pull on their boots, and set off along the trail that leads to the steep-faced sea cliffs, bays, inlets and rocky islets. A good road with plenty of parking runs out to overlook the Porta da Abra, while, on the way, a new roundabout marks the turning point to a spectacular viewing point (miradouro), where you may just find a local farmer selling produce from the back of a truck.

The Interior

If you look at the map on page 13, you see that Ribeira Brava is actually more centrally placed than Funchal, but it woefully lacks the commercial infrastructure of the capital. To the north the truly fantastic gorge fashioned by the river is lush in vegetation and followed, in the best serpentine manner of Madeiran mountain roads, by the old road. The pity is that there aren't many more viewing points where you can stop and take it all in. The road leads in splendid fashion to a high mountain pass, the Boca da Encumeada, although there is a quicker and lower option via a tunnel from the village of Serra de Agua – the high level route is infinitely more

Above: The vast, flat expanse of the Paúl da Serra is a mountain plain, a strong contrast to the jagged peaks of central Madeira. Here, at over 1300m, this is the largest flat part of the island, where little grows except ground-hugging plants and grass. Beyond its rim, the valley sides are flanked with lush laurissilva forests for which the island is renowned.

exciting, but really requires a clear day to get the best out of it. Just below the pass the Eucalipto Restaurant is a brilliant place to arrive just before lunch; the food is first-rate and varied in choice, and there is an impressive collection of Madeiran and Portuguese wines.

At the col, where there is a café and a small craft shop selling embroidery, wine and souvenirs, you either turn right and descend to São Vicente, or go left and climb steadily onto the magnificently flowered plateau of Paúl da Serra.

Paúl da Serra

Roughly translating as 'mountain plain', the Paúl da Serra, setting aside the display of modern wind turbines, is a delightfully empty and refreshing upland moor, possessed of splendid views. But it can be bleak, too, when mist shrouds the landscape; at over 1300m (4265ft) this is the largest flat part of the island, where little grows except ground-hugging plants and grass. Yet this is one of the

few places where you are likely to encounter cattle, being the only spot where it is safe for them to graze without the attendant risk of falling over a cliff edge. What may take you by surprise is the Estalagem Pico da Urze, a modern development of four-star hotel, shops, chapel and Jungle Rain café-restaurant. Specifically targeting walkers, this unexpected complex is ideally placed for anyone wanting to spend time walking the levadas of the Paúl da Serra without having to whizz up and down each day.

Although often clouded, the plateau can also be surprisingly clear of mist, which tends to drift downwards leaving the top of the island beautifully clear, and carpeted in summer with yellow and pink flowers. The whole area acts as a huge sponge for the rainwater that eventually emerges as springs all over the island. One place made endearingly romantic by such a spring is Rabaçal, on the western edge of the plateau. Here a very narrow, winding and steep road descends to a forest workers' hut in a lush glade, from where you can follow signs, eastwards, to the Levada do Risco and the lovely waterfall, the Cascata do Risco, where water cascades into a fern-draped amphitheatre and on down the tree-lined ravine of the Ribeira da Janela. This is all quite magical, almost fairytale-like, lichen drapes over tree branches, water tumbles merrily over rocks to make miniature waterfalls and the surrounding forest seems almost enchanted.

Estreito da Câmara de Lobos

Beyond Câmara de Lobos the road turns inland and winds energetically upwards through banana plantations and then vineyards to Estreito da Câmara de Lobos, a mountainside village overlooking the bay, and one of Madeira's key wine-producing areas. You come here for the view – quite splendid from the square in front of the 19th-century church – and arguably some of the finest Madeiran accommodation and dining on Madeira (*see* pages 112, 154). The shops, sadly, are filled with religious tat, but the village, normally a quiet, unassuming place, comes very much alive in September during the Madeira Wine Festival, when the harvest is celebrated with folk dancing, bare-foot wine pressing, and a certain amount of last year's sample testing.

Below: Terraced vineyards blanket the hillside above Câmara de Lobos, where the grape varieties sercial, verdelho, boal, malvasia and tinta negra mole are planted.

Jardim da Serra

Above Estreito da Câmara de Lobos the road winds up in desultory fashion to a place where the vines give way to cherry trees that are a delightful blossomy sight in springtime. Eventually, you reach the tiny hamlet of Jardim da Serra, a cluster of buildings, a few shops and houses.

But in June, when the cherries are ripe for picking, Jardim da Serra has its moment in the form of a cherry festival. As if by magic roadside bars appears, made from laurel branches, and the villagers put up clay ovens, stages and stands where you can buy chickens ready for the barbecue, beef cubed in readiness for the espetada, and tis, a light wine that you consume along with garlicky pork and dried fish. Of course, there are cherries too, available by the kilo, turned into liqueur, or baked into deliciously sticky cakes. Musicians liven the atmosphere and suddenly it's folk dancing until well after dark.

Close by is the Quinta do Jardim da Serra, sometime home of Henry Veitch, appointed by King George III as British Consul on Madeira. The quinta at Jardim da Serra was a house he particularly favoured, and so he surrounded it with plants and flowers from all over the world against a backdrop of forests and mountains.

Today it is a fine hotel and is still surrounded by a wealth of plants such as fuchsias, ferns, creepers and flowers, though much less than of old due to the unsympathetic design of an adjacent modern block. Veitch died in 1857, and lies buried on a small hill behind the house, where he used to sit looking down the valley.

Curral das Freiras

Commonly cited as one of the most vital places to visit while on Madeira, Curral das Freiras exceeds all expectations, especially if seen first from the viewing point at the very tip of a huge cliff (any suffering from vertigo should stay well back) overlooking this secret valley. This is surely one of the most spectacular locations on the island, set in a vast natural amphitheatre of rugged, perpendicular mountains, and it seems that the sole raison d'être of Eira do Serrado is to provide visitors with their first aerial glimpse of the village far below.

Long believed to be set in the crater of an extinct volcano (although this is disputed these days by geologists) the village dates from the 16th century, founded by nuns from Funchal, who fled the capital in 1566 following a devastating pirate attack when more than 1000 French freebooters ransacked Funchal over a period of 16 days. The nuns had traditionally farmed this

Left: Of all Madeira's riches, Curral das Freiras, or 'Nun's Valley', is arguably one of the most breathtaking, especially when viewed from the top of the massive cliff overlooking this hidden valley. This is one of the most spectacular locations on an island renowned for its spectacular settings.

inner hideaway, and for them it was a natural place of retreat; in time it became known as 'The Nun's Retreat', or Curral das Freiras. Sadly, there are no nuns today, nor any vestige of their convent, and the local people survive on a harsh agrarian economy and, increasingly, tourism. Life centres on the bars and cafés, and souvenir shops many of which sell craft items made by the person selling them to you.

At times the village can become overcrowded, and seem rather brash. But arrive early, maybe stay overnight at the Estalagem Eira do Serrado, and you won't be disappointed, but bear in mind that the sun doesn't reach the town until around midday.

The best way to reach Curral das Freiras is to come by car, for then it is that you can really appreciate the inaccessibility of the spot. Moreover, once you leave Eira do Serrado, you can follow the old road down to the village – a thin slice of serpentine highway clinging to precipitous cliffs, with two long, dark and damp tunnels to negotiate on the way. This is the way early travellers used to come, borne in hammocks slung on poles and carried by two strong young men. Until 50 years ago, it was the only way down.

Of course, it can all be avoided by using a modern tunnel that circumvents the ancient route, but the traditional way is a sensational experience, and the bars and cafés of the village a welcome sight at the end of it all. Energetic souls can walk down a zigzagging path from Eira do Serrado, reaching the village in approximately 45 minutes; the return journey is best done by bus, so check the timetable first, otherwise it will take two hours to climb back up.

This is one of those occasions when it is worth considering taking a taxi for the day; you can walk down from Eira do Serrado, and ask the taxi to meet you at the bottom.

The mountain slopes are cloaked in chestnut trees, so, not surprisingly, the village offers a range of chestnut cakes, soups, liqueur and steaks with chestnut sauce. In November there is a glorious chestnut festival to celebrate the harvest.

Pico do Arieiro

At an elevation of 1818m (5964ft), Pico do Arieiro is Madeira's third-highest mountain. Unlike the other mountains, this one can be reached by road from a junction along the mountain ridge at Poiso, and from the summit (complete with restaurant and bar), there is a stunning view across to Pico Ruivo, the high point of the island, west to the Paúl da Serra and east to the island of Porto Santo.

On the way, you pass a sign indicating the where-abouts of Poco de Neves, a curious, igloo-shaped structure built around 1800. This is an ice house, and before the days of refrigerators, ice was stored here to supply hospitals, and Reid's Hotel, where it found its way into gin and tonics. A spectacular, energetic and demanding walk links the two summits.

Porto Santo

The island of Porto Santo is much smaller than Madeira, having an area of only 42km² (16 sq miles), and, al-though anything but flat, having some rather shapely mountains of modest height, the island is quite arid. But what Porto Santo lacks in stature, it makes up for in a long swathe of fine sandy beach, something Madeira notably lacks. It has, too, its own microclimate which is generally better than Madeira, and, with very little rain-fall, attracts locals for weekend breaks.

For most of the year the 5000 or so inhabitants of Porto Santo have the place to themselves, with only the month of August bringing significant changes in the status quo when the Portuguese arrive in large number. The attraction, of course, is that sumptuous beach, 9km (almost 6 miles) of golden sand running the whole

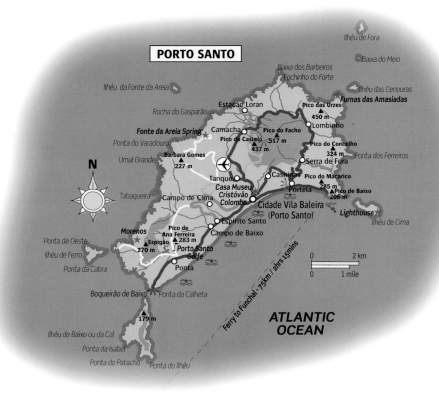

Above: Cidade Vila Baleira on Porto Santo, where Christopher Columbus once lived, is an attractive and bustling place of mainly 16th- and 17th-century buildings, with terracotta roofs and cobbled streets fringed by a range of exotic trees, shrubs and flowers, and facing directly onto the island's golden sands.

length of the southern coast from the main town and the island's capital, Cidade Vila Baleira, to Ponta da Calheta, overlooking the shapely Ilhéu de Baixo ou da Cal.

The best way of getting around, if you haven't brought your car on the ferry, is by bike, but you can, as on Madeira, book a taxi to take you around the island and show you the sights, many of which are quite stunning. Two of the island's summits are fairly easily climbed – Pico do Facho and Pico do Castelo. Morenos, the greenest oasis on the island is ideal for picnics, along with Fonte da Areia, the island's mini-spa.

Porto Santo is perfect for doing largely nothing, in an intentional and planned kind of way. It's a chilling-out

destination. But bird-watchers will find it especially rewarding: in the eight hours between arrival and heading back to the ferry port you can find rock sparrow, pipit, grey wagtail, sanderling, sandpiper, snipe, hoopoes and the occasional buzzard.

Christopher Columbus lived on Porto Santo for a time while married to Filipa Perestrelo, and his house, in Cidade Vila Baleira, is the only cultural attraction as such, the Casa Museu Cristóvão Colombo. But the island has a considerable history, and the centre of Cidade Vila Baleira reflects the passage of time with old buildings standing gable-to-gable with sleek, modern structures like the Congress Centre or the Arts and Crafts Centre.

But that is not why you come to Porto Santo; the sandy beach, relaxation and a lovely climate, are. But be warned, there is little in the way of natural shelter on the beach, so appropriate precautions against the heat and the sun are vital to a comfortable time. The waters that surround the island are warm and translucent, and swimming in them is every bit as enjoyable as feeling the

A Bit of History

According to the history books, Porto Santo was 'discovered' in 1418 by João Gonçalves Zarco and Tristão Vaz Teixeira, whom Prince Henry the Navigator had sent to explore the coast of Guinea. But a violent storm blew them off course, and they were swept westwards onto the sandy shores of an island, which in gratitude for their salvation they named Porto Santo (meaning 'safe' or 'holy port').

A wily Italian, Bartolomeu Perestrelo, joined them on their second journey a year later, and later became Governor of the island. Christopher Columbus, who came to Porto Santo in 1478 probably to see Perestrelo, met and married his daughter Filipa Moniz in 1479, but Filipa died soon after while giving birth to their son.

The discovery of Porto Santo was an important springboard to other discoveries along the west African coast, down to the Cape of Good Hope and from there to the East Indies and eventually the Far East.

golden sand sift between your toes. Diving is becoming increasingly important and popular in Porto Santo. As well as spear fishing off Porto de Abrigo, an old freighter has been sunk to create an artificial reef (*see* page 165). And if you really must get up and go, then jeep safaris are also an emerging trend, offering an individualistic, if bumpy way of seeing the island.

For golfing enthusiasts there is a fine 19-hole course on Porto Santo, the design of the Spanish golf supreme Severiano Ballesteros. Opened in 2004, this is not a course for novices, and is more challenging than the courses on Madeira, designed in marked contrast to the barren landscape that surrounds it. Complementing the golf, Porto Santo has a fine tennis complex that has already hosted several international tournaments, and offers an energetic alternative to the beach.

The main town, Cidade Vila Baleira, is an attractive and bustling place of mainly 16th- and 17th-century build-

ings, with terracotta roofs and cobbled streets fringed by a range of exotic trees, shrubs and flowers. The principal street, the Avenida Infante Dom Henrique leads down to that wonderful beach which is said to have healing qualities. So don't be surprised to find elderly people buried up to their necks in the sand – it's not some childish prank, but a genuine belief that the warm sands can cure ailments like eczema and varicose vein, as well as minor aches and pains.

In spite of its evident popularity, Porto Santo rarely feels crowded, and only then in and around Cidade Vila Baleira; elsewhere it has the relaxed air of a destination content to be what it is, unpretentious and calming.

Between Cicade Vila Baleira and the tip of the island at Ponta da Calheta lie a couple of scattered villages – Campo de Baixo and Cabeço da Ponta – with blocks of apartments, a few restaurants and hotels. This is a perfect location if all you want of your stay is to do nothing, or less. But this may change as plans exist for a big part of this stretch to be developed for tourism, including a casino.

At Ponta da Calheta the golden sand finally runs out, giving way to volcanic material; you can sit for hours at the Calhetas Restaurant watching the interaction between the sea and the rocks and the separate Ilhéu de Baixo ou da Cal. This is a delightful, mesmeric spot, but if you stay to watch the sun go down, then, unless staying overnight, you've missed your ferry back to Madeira.

In an hour you can easily drive round the central mass of mountains. Here the landscape really is barren and rugged, and a sharp contrast to the lush vegetation that covers Madeira. From directly above the bay there is a stunning view along the length of the beach, with a line of old windmills nearby.

Right: Porto Santo is significantly different from Madeira. While lush green vegetation predominates in Madeira, Porto Santo is barren in comparison. But the southern coast boasts a long and splendid beach of soft golden sand, which, with the island's mild climate, makes it a popular resort for day and longer visits.

Island Culture

Left: *August brings the Feast of the Assumption: island-wide celebrations with the biggest being at Monte. The twin-towered Church of Our Lady of Monte is a distinctive landmark from many parts of Funchal especially at night when the towers are illuminated.*

Since it was first inhabited, the topography of Madeira has precluded the development of a collective society, and proved more conducive to the development of isolated communities. Today, improving roads and popular culture have unified the island into a homogeneous whole, and such differences as remain are primarily those between Funchal and the so-called 'campo' (countryside).

By nature the natives of Madeira are farmers, the island having been originally settled by people from the Algarve. The farming of smallholdings is still the largest single economic activity outside of Funchal. Not surprisingly, many of the popular festivals around the island are linked to successful harvests of cherry, chestnut, sugar cane and, of course, grapes.

Left: Windmills, originally built to grind grain to make bread, are a typical sight in Porto Santo. The first windmill was built in 1794 and for many years these wood and stone structures have adorned the landscape of the island.

Early History

Those who chronicle the history of a place or an event invariably do so in a light most flattering to themselves. The history of Madeira is no exception, and which version of events you believe rather depends on your scepticism threshold. As ever, the truth lies buried in time.

The 15th century was a time of great exploration, nations were beginning to discover the world and the bounties it held. And few explorers were blind to the possibilities of favouritism and esteem that would befall them had they not only discovered new worlds, but, because it carried greater kudos, also survived perilous misadventure in the process. So it was with Captain João Gonçalves Zarco who, en route from Lisbon to Africa, was caught in a fierce storm which drove his ship off course. By the grace of God they were driven towards an 'undiscovered land', and named it Porto Santo (Holy Port) in thanksgiving. Returning to Portugal, Zarco reported sighting a much larger, cloud-covered island to the west, and was ordered to return and investigate, and to claim the new land, and Porto Santo, for Portugal.

Alas, as ever, reality has a way of diluting the romanticism of a tale. The islands, Porto Santo and the 'new'

Right: Much of Porto Santo is barren, as here around Pico de Macarico, but a forest reserve, with millions of trees planted, has been created to combat erosion. Already, in many places across Pico do Facho, Gandaia and Serra de Dentro a mantle of green is rapidly spreading.

	AD77	1351	1370	1418-1420	1425
Although it is easy to speculate that the islands of Madeira may have been populated long before the Portuguese colonists arrived, there is no evidence to support this.	Pliny the Elder refers in his Natural History to a group of islands off the African coast, which he called 'The Purple Islands'; these are believed to be the Madeiran archipelago.	The Madeiran archipelago appears on the Medici Map on which the names of the islands first appear: Porto Santo, Deserta and Isola de Lolegname.	An English merchant, Robert Machim, is shipwrecked on Madeira. His lover, Anne d'Arfet, died at the place that is today Machico, as did Machim himself. Machico is said to be named in their honour.	Madeira and Porto Santo are 'discovered' by João Gonçalves Zarco and Tristão Vaz Teixeira, and claimed for Portugal.	Madeira is declared a province of Portugal. Zarco is governor of the western half of the island, and founds Funchal.

1440	1446	1450	1452	1455	1478
Teixeira is put in charge of eastern Madeira, with Machico as its capital.	Porto Santo comes under the control of Bartolomeu Perestrelo, who is appointed governor.	Zarco becomes governor of western Madeira, with Funchal as the capital.	Sugar canes are first imported, and Madeira develops as the most important sugar supplies in Europe using slave labour imported from Africa and the Canary Islands.	The cultivation of vines begins.	Christopher Columbus, then a sugar merchant, is known to have visited Madeira.

would simply ignore it. Admittedly, Zarco had only one eye, having lost one at the Battle of Ceuta in Morocco in 1415, and was for ever thereafter known to his friends as Zarco the 'Squinter' or 'Cross-eyed'.

Most likely is the notion that the good captain, and his friend and ally Prince Henry 'the Navigator', heir to the Portuguese throne, already knew of the islands and realized how ideal they would be, given their proximity to favourable trade winds, as a staging post for Portuguese voyages of discovery to the real New World further west. The islands of Madeira appeared on maps well before Zarco and company came on the scene, and it is hard to believe that Prince Henry, the founder of the School of Seamanship, would not have been aware of this. The Medici Map of 1351 (today in the Laurentian Library in Florence), compiled by Genoese cartographers, and the Map of Macia de Viladeste of 1413, both show a group of islands off the African coast named as Porto Séo, Deserta and Isola de Lolegname, the latter translating as 'the wooded island'. This is the Italian translation for the Arab word 'El Aghnam', meaning island of timber, and suggests that the islands may first have been discovered by the Arabs. Of course, given the vagaries of 14th-century mapping techniques, the islands could equally have been the Azores or the Canary Islands, although the name similarities point to them being the Madeiran Islands. Pliny the Elder, the Roman writer (AD23–79), always an astute, if sometimes imaginative chronicler, mentions the islands in his Natural History

island to the west, were already known. Indeed, it is said that Zarco, or maybe other Portuguese sailors, would often visit what is today Madeira to gather resin from its dragon trees, later to be used as a dye. It is, after all, stretching credibility a little too far to accept that an adventurous captain supposedly within sight of some 'unknown' land, and with an eye to the main chance,

1497	1508	1514	1530	1566	1580
King Manuel I embraces Madeira into the Portuguese kingdom, makes Funchal the island's only capital, and appoints descendants of Zarco to be governor.	Funchal granted a town charter by King Manuel.	The population of Madeira, excluding slaves, is recorded as 5000; it is believed that there are just as many slaves, but these are not recorded.	Madeiran sugar trade decreases in the face of competition from America.	French pirates under the command of Bernard de Montluc attack Funchal, destroy churches and palaces, and massacre the garrison.	Portugal loses its independence to Spain, and King Philip II becomes sovereign of the Madeiran archipelago.

(AD77), calling them the 'Purple Islands'. Of course, this may be no more than an allusion to something hazy on the horizon, or, as has been suggested, it is a reference to the purple-red dye produced by the sap from the ubiquitous dragon trees. If Pliny's account is correct, then not only were the islands known long before the 14th century, but were quite possibly inhabited, too.

So, in 1419, Zarco set sail allegedly to claim Porto Santo, returning to 'conquer' Madeira a year later. Sadly, even this tempting nugget of historical story telling doesn't make logistical sense – why, having already supposedly been blown off course, make the long and potentially dangerous journey back to Portugal only to return a year later, when it would have been a simple matter of making a much shorter journey west to claim Madeira at the same time? Would it not have been more meritorious to return having victoriously discovered not one but two groups of islands?

Informed opinion today supports the notion that under the orders of Prince Henry, Zarco returned with Tristão Vaz Teixeira and Bartolomeu Perestrelo, and conveniently 'rediscovered' the islands. Certainly manuscripts that

Opposite: Statue of Christopher Columbus gazes out to sea from the Parque de Santa Catarina. Columbus, then a sugar merchant, visited Madeira in 1478. He lived for a time on Porto Santo.

Right: In 1918, the municipality of Funchal ordered that a monument in honour of Zarco be erected in celebration of the five hundred years since Madeira's discovery. The statue was completed ten years later.

1620	1640	1662	1801	1807	1851
Pirate John Ward plunders Funchal, and carries off 1200 people to sell as slaves.	Portugal regains its independence following a revolt against Spanish rule	Catherine of Bragança marries Charles II of England who gains important trading concessions for English merchants many of whom later settle in Madeira.	British troops use Madeira as base against the forces of Napoleon.	Start of seven-year occupation of Madeira by British, many of whom decide to stay and settle.	Wine harvests destroyed by mildew and vine pest; many inhabitants migrate.

chronicle the events, admittedly written 170 years after the event, record that Zarco found the islands uninhabited, but noticed that there were signs of previous occupants in the valley of Machico.

For reasons that are poorly explained, Zarco's action on reaching Madeira was to set it ablaze, ostensibly to clear land for colonization. So fiercely did the land burn that according to one account map makers seven years later reported their inability to complete their tasks because the fire was still raging. It all seems far fetched, and may smack of an early episode of opportunistic spin doctoring, passing off small-scale burning that got out of control, as a planned clearance of a much larger area on which to grow cereals, which Portugal lacked, and to endorse Portugal's maritime expansion.

Having claimed Madeira and Porto Santo for Portugal, Zarco was made Governor of western Madeira in 1450 with control over half of the entire island, having been made Captain of Funchal in 1425, while his allies, Tristão Vaz Teixeira and Bartolomeu Perestrelo, shared the remaining half and Porto Santo from 1440 and 1446 respectively. During this time, it was Machico rather than Funchal that was the capital of the islands; Funchal (named after the wild fennel that grew there in great

Left: This fine azulejo depicting the Monte toboggan run also illustrates the old railway that once linked Monte and Terreiro da Luta. Plans are afoot to reinstate this old railway as a tourist attraction.

1856	1860	1891	1916	1921	1947
A cholera epidemic kills almost 10,000 inhabitants.	An Englishwoman, Miss Phelps, introduces embroidery to Madeira, generating a new source of income for the island.	Reid's Hotel opens in Funchal, initiating popularity among aristocracy of Europe.	Having declared war on Portugal, Germany attacks Madeira, shelling Funchal from U-boats.	The first trip from Lisbon to Funchal takes place on 22 March, on a hydroplane, Type F3, no. 4018 S606 'Rolls Royce'.	British seaplanes begin the first scheduled flights to Madeira.

Statistics

Madeira

Area: 798km² (307 sq miles)

Size: 57km (35 miles) east-west; 22km (14 miles) north-south

Population: 245,000, with more than 40% living in Funchal.

Language: Portuguese

Currency: Euro

Religion: Roman Catholic

Government: Autonomous Administrative Region within the Republic of Portugal.

Porto Santo

Area: 42km² (16 sq miles)

Size: 11km (7 miles) long, and 5km (3 miles) wide.

Population: 4800

quantities) only emerging as the main centre in the early 16th century, largely due to its better anchorage and the granting of a town charter in 1508.

Early Settlement

Once Madeira and Porto Santo were securely in the Portuguese bag, so to speak, colonization was to follow swiftly, starting with the Portuguese nobility, who acquired large tracts of land. During the years that fol-

lowed an influx of work people, labourers and craftsmen came from mainland Portugal, and huge areas of land were subjected to cereal production, much of it exported either to mainland Portugal or Portuguese trading posts. But by the end of the 15th century, the cultivation of sugar cane had taken over, the back-breaking cultivation of virgin land largely undertaken by slaves and convicts. This was a period of great economic and cultural development; Madeira was acquiring an identity that was to become known throughout the civilized world. Yet it is estimated that more than half its population were slaves, a huge workforce of whom there is no place in Madeira's recorded history other than in a few street names. But the legacy of their labours remains in the great carved terraces that line the valley sides, and, ironically now proving one of the great attractions to Madeira, the vast network of water channels, the levadas.

But prosperity was not to last. Competition from Brazil, sugar cane diseases, and a reduction in soil fertility heralded a 17th-century crisis in social and economic well-being, not helped by the attentions of French, English and Moorish pirates during the 16th century, notably John Ward who plundered Funchal and carried off 1200 people to be sold as slaves in Tunisia.

Over the years, all sorts of people came to Madeira, from rogues and vagabonds to princes and lesser nobility, not least Henrique Alemão, exiled king of Poland, who fled his homeland after defeat in the Battle of Varna in 1444. A great many were dispossessed knights from

1964	1974	1982	1986	1997	1999
Funchal airport opened, heralding mass tourism.	The great revolution; soldiers overthrow the postwar dictatorship and pave the way for democracy.	Madeira's regional government declares two-thirds of the island a natural reserve – the Parque Natural da Madeira. The protected area also includes the laurissilva forests, the Desertas and the Selvagens islands, the Natural Reserve of Garajau, and the Natural Reserve of Rocha do Navio.	Portugal's membership of the European Union enables development funds to be directed to Madeira's infrastructure, enabling electricity and roads to be supplied to remote rural communities.	The new south coast motorway opens on Madeira, transforming travel on the island.	The Madeira Nature Reserve, which largely comprises the laurissilva forests are designated as a UNESCO World Heritage Site.

The Last Austrian Emperor

Karl I (1887–1922), Karl Franz Josef Ludwig Hubert Georg Maria von Habsburg-Lothringen, was the last Emperor of Austria, the last King of Hungary and Bohemia, and the last monarch of the Habsburg Dynasty. He reigned as Emperor Karl I of Austria, King Charles III of Bohemia and King Charles IV of Hungary from 1916 until 1918, when he renounced the government (but did not abdicate). Karl spent the remaining years of his life in exile on Madeira (after first trying to settle in Switzerland) attempting to regain the throne. While staying at Reid's Hotel, he and his wife accepted the generous offer of a Portuguese aristocrat to move to Quinta do Monte. But already a sickly man, he died in 1922 of severe pneumonia after walking into Funchal on a freezing winter's day. Many Roman Catholics saw him as a saint, and his canonization was formally proposed in 1949.

Right: Santa Catarina, Madeira's airport, began life as an experimental airport in 1957. The extension of the airport runway in 2000 was the largest engineering work ever carried out on Madeira. Today, the airport can handle regular Airbus flights, and in 2004 won the World Award for Structural Engineering.

ence to Spain, when King Philip II became sovereign of the Madeiran archipelago. Independence was restored only in 1640, and followed in 1662 by the marriage of Catarina de Bragança and Charles II after the Restoration of the English monarchy. But for a patriotic act of omission, Madeira may well have become a British possession at this time. It was certainly intended as part of her dowry, but was deftly overlooked in the marriage contract – that the guilty scribe was a Madeiran leaves little need for explanation, astute though his actions were.

The Jesuits

In 1566, when pirates under the command of Bertrand de Montluc occupied Funchal, a call for help was despatched to mainland Portugal. The response from Lisbon came too late to help, but on board the ships was a group of Jesuit priests, intended to offer succour and consolation to the devastated population. When the ships returned to Portugal, the Jesuits remained, preaching and spreading their religion among a receptive people. So grateful were the Madeiran people, that they petitioned the king to establish a Jesuit college on the

Portugal to whom King João I granted land on which to build a new life, and invested their unmarried daughters with a sense of patriotic duty to marry and breed a new race of island Portuguese. The occurrence of many surnames – Henriques, Freitas and Almeida – that would in Portugal be recognized as deriving from aristocratic families is testimony to the zeal with which the king's wishes were observed.

For a time, Portugal and Madeira lost their independ-

SANTA CATARINA AIRPORT: 1957	1964	1972	1973	1975
A plane lands for the first time on the ground of Madeira Island, on an experimental runway in Santa Catarina. It was a small aircraft of the General Directorate of Civil Aeronautics.	On 8 July the airport service of Madeira becomes complete as Santa Catarina Airport starts to function. On the first commercial flight (8 July), aboard a Dakota CS-DGA, there are 80 arrivals and 66 departures.	First thoughts are given to providing Madeira with an intercontinental airport.	A new terminal replaces the first one, now prepared to host 500,000 passengers per year.	Two foreign companies – Dixon Spies Association and The Economist Int. Unit – begin a study into the building of an intercontinental airport on Madeira.

island, a request that was treated favourably. The first college was built on Largo do Chafariz, although they soon moved from there. In 1599, they acquired two quintas away from Funchal, farming the land and cashing in on the growing wine trade by introducing two new grape varieties to the island – sercial and verdelho.

Regarded as enemies by the Marquês de Pombal, the Jesuits were expelled from Madeira in 1760; their church and college buildings on the north side of Praça do Municipio, left derelict only to see service in the 19th century as a military barracks, and later as part of the university.

1975	1982–1986	2000	2002	2004
Dixon Spies Association studies 15 areas that at a first glance offer better conditions for the functioning of an infrastructure of intercontinental character: Ponta do Pargo, Ponta São Lourenço, Santo Amaro, São Martinho, Prazeres, São Jorge, Santana, Porto da Cruz, Caniçal, Camacha, Câmara de Lobos, Porto Moniz, Santo da Serra, Paul da Serra and Caniço. No doubt those locations breathed a sigh of relief when it was concluded that Santa Catarina in Santa Cruz was still the best place.	The runway, initially of 1600 metres, is extended to 1800 metres. The aircraft platform is also enlarged from five to nine parking places. The extension of the airport runway is the largest engineering work ever undertaken on Madeira.	The runway is further extended to 2781 metres. As a work of extreme technical complexity, the runway is partially built in flagstone above the sea, on a backfill created to withstand the 180 pillars that support the new part of Runway 23.	Opening of the new passenger terminal, with 40 check-in counters, 16 boarding gates, three rolling carpets for departure luggage and four more for arrivals.	The extension of the runway wins the 'World Award for Structural Engineering'.

Above: William Reid's great hotel, formerly a quinta, is perched on rocky cliffs above the bay of Funchal, and has long been the principal hotel in the capital. It was here that Churchill stayed in the late 1940s.
Previous page: Terraced vineyards and fruit plantations dominate the sloping terrain of Madeira, and are increasingly found in most parts of the island.

The British in Madeira

British presence in Madeira began as the wine trade flourished, but came about mainly as a result of the Napoleonic Wars of the early 19th century when British troops arrived to protect Madeira. Many British explorers and travellers also settled here and decided to stay, beguiled by the island's charm and comfortable climate, and giving rise to a virile and cosmopolitan community of landowners and traders.

Mass tourism was to come only with the building of the island's airport in 1964, but much earlier than this saw the arrival, in 1836, of the son of a Scottish crofter, William Reid. With William Wilkinson, Reid availed himself of the opportunities afforded by setting up an agency to cater for well-heeled visitors coming in search of Madeiran delights, among which the milder climate was paramount. Many planned long stays, up to six months, and sought to rent independent houses with gardens (quintas) which they furnished to their own tastes. Before long Reid was making enough money to begin buying the quintas for himself, and turn them into hotels. His great prize, today Reid's Palace Hotel, was the quinta of Dr Michael Grabham, perched high on the clifftop overlooking Funchal.

The issues of health were not least among the reasons for accepting Reid's hospitality. The climate was deemed perfect for those afflicted by maladies such as respiratory disease, tuberculosis, nervous disorders and heart conditions. Exasperation and boredom with Austrian court life may not, however, have a clinical definition, but may well have been the true explanation of the 'fevers' endured by Princess Elizabeth, wife of Emperor Franz Joseph who came to Madeira in search of 'improvement'.

In the early 20th century, the Germans almost succeeded in gaining possession of Madeira where Britain had failed. An altruistic 'plan' to build a group of hospitals on the

The Legend of Robert Machim

The legend of Robert Machim and Anne d'Arfet, originated between the years 1328 and 1346, just as the Hundred Years' War was beginning. Edward III was king of England, and one of his noblemen, named 'Dorset', 'Hereford' or 'Arfet' had a beautiful daughter, Anne, who had an illicit love affair with Robert Machim, a humble worker from a poor family and very much a man beneath her station. Marriage between the two was not permitted for social, political and family reasons, and Anne was ordered by the Court to marry a man much her senior, a squire of the Court; Machim was put behind bars. But he escaped and fled to London to find Anne, and together they took flight, eloping in the night, and embarked from Bristol on a journey to France (some accounts say that Spain was their destination, and, having regard to what followed, this seems the more likely).

During the voyage a storm blew them off course, and they drifted, helpless, for many days until finally cast ashore on some unknown land, in a small bay at the bottom of a beautiful valley, where they took shelter. Anne was weak from her ordeal, and after just three days in this strange land she died. Robert Machim, filled with sorrow and desolation died just five days later; the two of them were buried side by side in the place today called Machico.

And so the legend of Robert Machim came to be inscribed in many literary works, although how much of the conflicting details that have descended across the years is near the truth will never be known.

island by a company headed by Prince Frederick Karl Höhenlohe, on terms that would vest Germany with the power to control the island's affairs, was rumbled only at the eleventh hour, when it was realized that the so-called hospitals were fundamentally a chain of hotels.

In 1974 came the greatest revolution of all, when Madeira was declared an Autonomous Political Region, ending Portugal's fifty-year dictatorship and introducing democracy. Since 1976, Madeira has been governed by the Popular Social Democratic Party under the charismatic figure of Alberto João Jardim who has ruled like a king in all but name.

The Slave Trade

It would be convenient to overlook the role of slaves in the rise of Madeira, but to do so would render a grave injustice to the many people who were responsible for much of the island's history and culture.

As with most places, Madeiran slaves were captured, usually by violent means, in this instance mainly from Africa. Warfare was the most common method, with the vanquished being sold into enslavement. During the 15th century, the Portuguese were keen to explore Africa and needed labour to work on the irrigation system, the levadas, of Madeira, which were to carry water to the crops. And so it was that the first slaves arrived in 1452: Moors, Berbers and Guanches, natives of the Canary Islands.

Slave labour was used for the back-breaking work of building the levadas, much of which was both difficult and

Below: Although the island has its own flag, Madeira remains firmly attached to Portugal, and the Portuguese flag is a common sight across the island.

perilous, with the slaves often hanging from baskets over the steep cliffs. Not surprisingly, many lost their lives, falling to their deaths. By 1552 there were more than 5000 slaves on Madeira, and many were moved to working in the sugar mills. A little earlier than this, Pope Pius III, whose predecessor, Pius II, had decreed that no baptized African should be enslaved, began voicing concern about the condition in which slaves were kept. But the slave trade was to continue for another 200 years, only ending in November 1767, when a ship anchored off Funchal with 300 slaves aboard was prohibited from off-loading its human cargo. Before then slaves were treated as human stock and sold by weight. Portuguese law allowed the branding of slaves to prove ownership, cutting off ears for minor offences, and subjecting them to an evening curfew.

The legacy of the African slaves lives on: while the Portuguese were busy setting up their new order and society, the African slaves maintained their own culture and cuisine with a tenacity that withstood the years of enslavement. Many of today's popular dishes in the Madeiran cuisine have Arabic links, like the espetada, the meat kebabs, and milho, a type of polenta made from corn meal, one of the lasting culinary vestiges of slavery.

Long after slavery was abolished, their influence can be traced in the music and folk dancing of Madeira, most noticeably the form of dancing in a circle with bowed heads, which has clear African origins. Undoubtedly, slavery everywhere was a dark period for mankind, no less so in Madeira than elsewhere. But, equally, a by-product of slavery has been an enrichment of the culture and heritage of island Madeira.

The People of Madeira

The greater number of Madeiran people today are of Portuguese origin, descendants of 15th-century settlers who came to the island from Alentejo and the Algarve. They are a friendly, welcoming people, not as volubly outgoing as people from, say, Spain or Italy, but possessed of a quiet pride in their island community. This is a deeply conservative society, one that enjoys the traditional family values and those of the Roman Catholic

Above: *This accordion player in the traditional dress of Madeira provides entertainment in the hill village of Monte, but folk groups often visit the Funchal hotels to provide evenings of light entertainment and fun.*

church, to which the vast majority demonstrate some measure of allegiance. Yet, as with most countries, the younger element, better educated, better informed, aware of a wider world and of world issues, are questioning the old ways, the old traditions; not to any significantly detrimental degree, but just enough for it to spill over into a quest for something 'other'.

The Way of Life

Given the relative glamour and glitz (such as it is) of Funchal, it would be easy to be lured into thinking of Madeira as a virile, energetic, progressive society, upwardly mobile in the world. And in good measure it is; a massive road construction programme is in place and new apartment blocks are being built alongside more hotels for tourists. But land is at a premium; on the slopes above Funchal, houses are shoe-horned into available space, old, poor quality houses are being pulled down – just before they fall down – and new properties fed into the vacuum. Moreover, land is required for what sustainable farming can be carried out if the island isn't going to become wholly dependent on imported goods. Nor is all the land suitable for farming; much of it is barren and rocky, parched earth. So what land there is, is carefully tended.

Travel away from Funchal, into the mountain villages, and another story emerges; one that is not quite so affluent, one that is more needy, more dependent these days on tourism. It can be a pitiful sight to see an elderly woman teetering up a hill slope beneath a heavy burden of hay, or another by the roadside baking bread. But that is a reality of life in rural Madeira. And it is the celebration of that way of life that becomes most evident in the calendar of yearly festivals and celebrations, a time-honoured observance of more fundamental things. Perhaps it is the celebration of the wine or chestnut harvests, or a local saint's day. Equally, it may be the commemoration of some miraculous event or a date in history that muscles in on the year's partying. In this manner, the old way of life and its traditional values lives on. Folk music and dancing, too, are part of that culture, and many of the hotels have 'Folk Evenings', when dancers in traditional costumes will visit, dance and sing, and engage diners in a little harmless revelry. All dancers, some very young it is pleasing to see, wear traditional

Below: Roadside bread makers are a common sight outside Funchal. Bolo do Caco, a local speciality, is a round, flat bread, made with wheat flour and cooked on a tile. Spread with garlic butter and eaten hot they are delicious.

Madeiran folk costume: baggy trousers, white shirt and ponderous boots (for the men), and white blouse, with an embroidered cape, usually in red, but sometimes black, a waistcoat and a long, multicoloured striped skirt (for the women). Both men and women wear a carapuca, or skull-cap with a twirled point, and perform to the accompaniment of a rajão or braguinha (a cross between a small guitar and a mandolin), castanholes (castanets), drum, a raspadeiro (a notched stick played rather like a skiffle washboard), and a ring of cloth puppets attached to a stick, a brinquinho, which jangles as the stick is thumped rhythmically on the ground. Of course, it's simply entertainment, and some may see it as demeaning the island culture. But each dance, each song, has meaning and sig-

Below: Embroidery is a prized souvenir of visits to Madeira, both for its beauty and exquisite detail. It can be found in many forms, from tablecloths to handkerchiefs.

nificance for the people of Madeira, and in re-enacting that meaning, it is also preserving it for posterity.

Plaintive and often dramatic, the Madeiran form of singing known as fado, has its roots in Portugal, and tells of unrequited love or some other equally painful life event. Originating in the beer houses of Lisbon, and usually accompanied by a guitarist, fado may well be one of those lingering associations with African slaves. You can hear fado at many places, but the most popular is Arsenio's in Funchal Old Town.

Traditional Crafts
Embroidery and Tapestry

Originally the preserve of Portuguese aristocracy, the art of embroidery, known as bordados, came to Madeira with the first settlers. It has since become a cottage industry, but one that has to compete with cheap imports from the Far East. In many of the rural villages, however, hand-

Above: Wickerwork can be seen and bought in many markets in Funchal but especially in Camacha, which has become the main wickerwork centre for the island. Here you can visit wickerwork warehouses and buy anything from a baby's crib to a three-piece suite.

crafted needlework of one form or another can still be found, and often purchased from the person who made it. All of the large items will carry some form of seal of authenticity from IBTAM, the Institute of Embroidery, Tapestry and Handicrafts. But absence of the seal does not necessarily mean that the item has been imported; one young woman in Curral das Freiras offered to make two small doilies while we watched, to make up the four we wanted. That's authentic, seal or no seal. But it is a valid warning that much of what poses as authentic is imported, not only from the Far East but from Portugal, too.

The Núcleo Museológico do IBTAM, the museum centre of the Madeiran Institute for Embroidery, Tapestry and Handicrafts on the Rua do Visconde de Anadia in Funchal contains a fine collection of 19th- and early 20th-century embroidered cloths and decorative pieces, illustrating the décor in the homes of fine Madeiran families during the Romantic era.

The craft of embroidering is quite painstaking, but the institute offers an easy and informative insight into the skills involved.

Wickerwork

After embroidery, wickerwork (vimes) is the second most important handicraft on Madeira. It was a British sugar merchant, William Hinton, who saw the commercial possibilities of wickerwork in the 1850s, and started supplying the hugely fashionable cane furniture to hotels. Camacha is the main place to find wickerwork, although you will need to scour the side streets to find men working away at an item. Even so, there are over 2000 of them, and wickerwork provides a hidden benefit too, to the farmers around Boaventura on the north coast, from where most of the willow wands come.

The Culture of Madeira

To understand a nation of people, you first need to understand its history and its culture. In Madeira, in Funchal especially, it is impossible to escape that history; it is around every corner, in the old churches and fantastic architecture, in the designs along the cobbled streets, in the decorative tiles that adorn so many walls, and increasingly in the museums that are evolving to record for posterity every element of the island's history.

As you tour the island, you encounter monuments that are part of the archipelago's history, and statues that acknowledge the debt of modern Madeira to the early explorers and settlers, people like João Gonçalves Zarco on the Avenida Arriaga, and Christopher Columbus who gazes out to sea from the Parque de Santa Catarina.

Many of the seigniorial mansions of former times, known as quintas, and once the homes of princes and noblemen, have been converted to luxurious accommo-

***Below:** 'Quintas' like the Quinta de Bela Vista, offer a lifestyle of refinement, quality and luxury, and the elegance of palaces; they are often surrounded by beautiful gardens and lakes. These former homes of aristocratic families, embody the history of old Madeira, but with a very modern emphasis on luxury and good taste.*

dation, while retaining the core element of their historic designs (*see* page 100). One such, below the mountain village of Monte, is the Monte Palace, and although the palace is not open to the public, the botanical garden that surrounds it certainly is (*see* page 23). Within the grounds one building houses a fascinating museum – the Monte Palace Museum – where a vast collection of sculptures originating from Zimbabwe's Tengenenge region is on view. Much of the collection is made up of works from the first generation of artists from Tengenenge, created between the 1950s and 1960s.

The Madeira Story Centre
Located at the edge of the Old Town in Funchal in a former cinema on Rue D. Carlos, the Madeira Story Centre vividly portrays the history of Madeira in a series of interactive audiovisual sections, each embracing a clear-cut period in the development of Madeira, compressing 14 million years into a matter of minutes.

This is an exhibition that will appeal to children, but will also prove useful to visitors who want the encapsulated version of the island's history.

Wine Museums
The Museum of Madeira Wine, found in the Madeira Wine Institute (Instituto do Vinho da Madeira) on Rua 5 de Outubro – is the official authority for quality control of Madeira wine, the ultimate authority, in fact, in matters concerning Madeiran wine. The building once belonged to Henry Veitch (*see* panel, page 48), the English consul to Madeira during the first half of the 19th century. The architecture of the building, with its prominent watch tower, is enough reason to visit and enjoy this rather discreet museum. Designed by Veitch himself, it eventually became a prototype for consular buildings in other countries.

This small museum offers an instructive approach to Madeira wine: its history, method of production, barrel making, export markets, and just plain old nostalgia. Commendably, the museum focuses on areas that receive little attention when Madeira wine is mentioned

Madeira Wine in a Nutshell
Madeira is a fortified wine made by a special heating process that warms the wine over a prolonged period. It comes in a variety of styles, ranging from dry to very sweet, and the best examples are capable of ageing almost indefinitely.

Once opened, a bottle of Madeira, resistant to oxidization, will stay fresh for many weeks, even months, although the blended wines age rather less gracefully than single vintage. You can expect to find complex flavours of nuts, caramel and raisins, and all the things wine buffs talk about. But at the end of the day, it is eminently drinkable, on virtually any occasion.

Expect to pay around 15€ for the cheapest brand, and considerably more, rising to 150€+ for a top vintage wine, if you're that way inclined.

So popular did Madeira wine become that by the time of the English king Charles II, demand for Madeira was firmly established along the North American seaboard. Indeed, the wine came to play such a central part in the American way of life that it was used to toast the Declaration of Independence and the Inauguration of George Washington (first President of the United States) who, it was said, 'drank a pint of Madeira at dinner daily.'

in visitor guides or books: the types of wood used for barrels, the types and methods of early wine presses, the casks, sheep or goatskins, or bullock cart modes of transportation of times past.

The Madeira Wine Museum is housed in a former Franciscan monastery, a series of Baroque buildings on the Avenida Arriaga where the wine used to be stored and sold. The museum's collection includes documents from the British companies that founded the Madeira Wine Company. The origins of the company lie in 1913 when Welsh & Cunha and Henriques & Camara, two developing wine companies joined forces to form the Madeira Wine Association. In later years more companies joined to ensure their survival by reducing costs and pooling production whilst maintaining commercial independence. Blandy's and Leacock's, two of the most important British companies, amalgamated their interests and joined the association in 1925.

The museum is certainly one of the most atmospheric; a cluster of old buildings round a cobbled central courtyard with banana and palm trees that was once a medieval street. The original and well-kept interiors and equipment have been preserved to offer an authentic environment in which to have a 'Taste and Buy' experience. There is a 17th-century lagar (an early wine press) from Porto Santo, along with instruments of the trade, including a token working cooperage, measuring tools and historical labels. The lingering aroma of wine and resting wooden barrels is hugely evocative of another age, and shamefully conducive to a little imbibing.

Museu da Baleia (Whale Museum), Caniçal

Madeira has a long history of whaling, and the Whale Museum in the small fishing village of Caniçal looks back at the whaling activities that for decades formed a vital part of fishermen's lives. Whaling has been prohibited in Madeiran waters since 1982, so today many of the sailors who once harpooned whales for a living are working to help preserve these beautiful and gentle giants of the ocean.

The visual exhibit ranges from pictures of the preparation of boats, whale spotting on the high sea and hunting methods to and images of festivities after a successful hunt. There are other pictures showing the processing and transport of processed whale material, including oil extraction and meat preparation.

CULTURAL SIGHTS IN MADEIRA

A major attraction of the museum is the model of a life-size sperm whale alongside which is a tiny fishing boat, similar to those used by the whale hunters, showing just how dangerous the process of catching whales was and how imminently the fishermen were in danger of being capsized.

The Museum of Natural History

The Museum of Natural History (Museu de História Natural) is located in the botanical gardens (Jardim Botânico) on the western hillside of the Funchal amphitheatre.

The museum, opened in 1982, is the legacy of Ernesto João Smith – a Jesuit priest and eminent ornithologist, and contains many species of the flora and fauna of the Madeiran archipelago, including deep-sea specimens from the ocean floor, as well as numerous specimens that are not recorded anywhere else in the world. The

Left: The Madeira Botanical Gardens are among Madeira's most treasured tourist attractions. Within an area of 80,000 square metres is ranged a truly fascinating collection of more than 2500 plant species. Located in the amphitheatre above Funchal, the gardens provide spectacular panoramic views over the mountainous backdrop, the city below and its bay.

collection also includes rare species that may be facing extinction, as well as examples of fauna endemic to Madeira and Porto Santo.

This is one of the most agreeable museums to visit, located as it is in the expansive botanical gardens, which house thousands of examples of flora from many parts of Macaronesia.

Artistic Impressions

It is by no means surprising to find paintings by the Flemish Masters on display in Madeira's museums. Once, these beautiful pictures graced the island's chapels, but today they are available for all to see in the Museum of Sacred Art in Funchal, housed in what used to be the Old Episcopal Court of Funchal, in Rua do Bispo (Bishop's Road), and first opened to the public in 1955. The museum building was built over two significant periods: the 16th century, when the Saint Louis chapel was built along with the balcony and arches that face out onto the lovely Praça do Município; the second period of development came during the reconstruction process in the 18th century following the devastation of the 1748 earthquake. Major adaptations were made to the building's structure between 1942 and 1955 to accommodate the new museum with its cache of paintings, sculptures and jewellery. Most of the pieces on display are from the 16th and 17th centuries, including Portuguese, Flemish, and Madeiran works. It is the paintings that most attract visitors to the museum: which offers one of the most complete single collections of painted wooden boards of the Flemish School of Art.

Flemish Art

How did so many valuable Flemish works of art arrive on the distant shores of Madeira? The answer lies in the wealth generated by sugar cane production in the 16th and 17th centuries. Huge fortunes were made as sugar was a valuable and much sought after commodity in Europe. The wealth amassed made it possible for merchants to donate many of their works of art to the Church.

Much of Madeira's art has been the work of visiting artists. Sir Winston Churchill remains a renowned visitor to the island of Madeira, one who loved to paint.

Porta 33

At the end of the 20th century, Madeiran art was almost dormant, and part of the problem was that Madeira never had a major exhibition centre. Enter Porta 33 on the Rua do Quebra Coastas in Funchal (www.porta33.com), an art gallery destined to put Madeira not only on the art map of Portugal, but of Europe also.

One key feature that makes Porta 33 individual, is its philosophy of requiring its exhibiting artists to travel to Madeira to ensure a more productive collaboration between artist and gallery. Artists were also invited to extend their stay and to create 'site-specific' works relating their experience of the island. This has had the effect of enabling the presentation of new and unseen work, and captured aspects of Madeira's place in contemporary culture, such as the traditional embroidery and wicker industries.

Elsewhere, the Quinta das Cruzes, the Frederico de Freitas Museum, and several other museums in Funchal are the places where many of the artistic and historical artefacts of the island's culture are to be found.

Left: The Museum of Sacred Art is renowned for its collection of Flemish works, like this painting of St Peter, by an unknown Flemish artist.

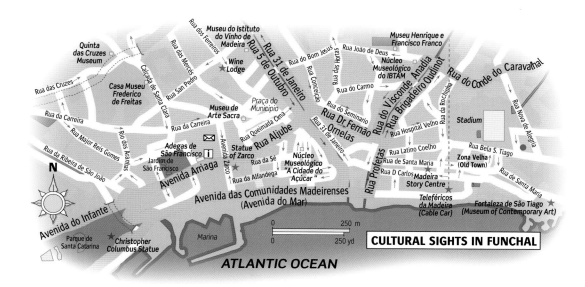

Museu do Istituto do Vinho de Madeira · Rua dos Ferreiros · Rua das Mercês · Rua 31 de Janeiro · Rua 5 de Outubro · Rua do Bom Jesus · Rua João de Deus · Museu Henrique e Francisco Franco · Quinta das Cruzes Museum · Wine Lodge · Rua das Hotas · Rua Conceição · Rua do Carmo · Núcleo Museológico do IBTAM · Rua do Visconde Anadia · Rua do Brigadeiro Oudinot · Rua do Conde do Caravalhal · Calçada de Santa Clara · Rua San Pedro · Casa Museu Frederico de Freitas · Praça do Municipio · Museu de Arte Sacra · Rua do Seminario · Rua Dr Fernão Ornelas · Rua da Rochinha · Stadium · Rua Nova de Alegria · Rua da Carreira · Rua da Carreira · Rua 31 de Janeiro · Rua Hospital Velho · Rua Major Reis Gomes · Rio dos Aranhas · Avenida Zarco · Rua Queimada Cma · Rua Aljube · Statue of Zarco · Rua da Sé · Núcleo Museológico "A Cidade do Açúcar" · Rua Latino Coelho · Rua Bela S. Tiago · Adegas de São Francisco · Jardim de São Francisco · Rua de Santa Maria · Zona Velha (Old Town) · Rua da Ribeira de São João · Avenida Arriaga · Rua da Alfandega · Rua Projecta · Rua D Carlos I · Madeira Story Centre · Rua de Santa Maria · N · Avenida das Comunidades Madeirenses (Avenida do Mar) · Teleféricos da Madeira (Cable Car) · Fortaleza de São Tiago (Museum of Contemporary Art) · Avenida do Infante · Parque de Santa Catarina · Christopher Columbus Statue · Marina · ATLANTIC OCEAN · 250 m · 250 yd · **CULTURAL SIGHTS IN FUNCHAL**

Quinta das Cruzes

The Baroque-style Quinta das Cruzes on Calçada do Pico in Funchal opened in 1952 as one of the most prestigious museums on Madeira. It houses a splendid collection of antiques that are the legacy of the private collector César Gomes. In 1966 the collection was augmented by the addition of the private collection of fine and valuable decorative items of John Wetzler, a Czech citizen who resided on Madeira.

The combined donations of these philanthropists reveal a remarkable collection of uniquely Madeiran relics and antiques, notably porcelain, furniture made from rare woods, glazed pottery, marble, and cutlery. The collection is all the more important because it portrays the old Madeiran noble way of life, and helps us to understand the etiquette customs of the 16th to 19th centuries on Madeira, showing the visitor in typical fashion the way any fine lord or gracious nobleman would have lived on the island. The furnishings include Regency consoles, and chairs designed by the English cabinet-makers Chippendale and Hepplewhite.

The old mansion dates from the early period of colonization and was the home of the second Donee General of Funchal as his official residence. The surrounding archaeological garden contains many commemorative tombstones dating from the 15th to 19th centuries, and there is a fine orchid garden and nursery, with species collected and grown from endemic plants of Madeira.

Some of the furniture displays Renaissance through to Romantic craftsmanship and woodwork made in the 17th century from Madeiran wood by highly skilled craftsmen. Indo-Portuguese desks date from the 16th century along with English and Portuguese furniture from the 17th to 19th centuries.

A unique point of interest are the several Manueline windows (a style of architecture which flourished in Portugal during the reign of King Manuel I (1495–1521),

Following page: The Quinta das Cruzes has a splendid garden with archaeological sculptures. Focal points of the garden are the 16th-century Manueline windows carved out of basalt. In a quite compact setting you find the old manor house, today a museum for decorative arts and furniture, a chapel, the archaeological garden, the orchid cultivation, camphor trees, dragon trees, and eucalyptus from Australia.

Winston Churchill in Madeira

Winston Churchill is renowned for his excellent statesmanship during the Second World War. But he was well known in England before that time as a war correspondent for the Morning Post during the Second Boer War.

He visited Madeira in October 1899 on his way to South Africa, but half a century on, following election defeat in 1945, and a minor stroke in 1949, he came back to Madeira, seeking somewhere 'warm, paintable, bathable, comfortable and flowery', and a place where he could continue writing his memoirs.

Special preparations were to be made for Churchill's voyage. Madeira was to be not only a vacation, but also the place of his recuperation from the fatigue and ill health he had recently suffered.

Not in the best of health, Churchill wanted to elude the brouhaha of politics. While in Madeira, he stayed at Reid's Hotel, and travelled about in a grey Rolls Royce owned by the wine merchant family, Leacocks.

Alas, Churchill's stay in Madeira was a brief one: Clement Attlee, the post-war prime minister declared a new election date, prompting an early return for Churchill for what was to be yet another electoral defeat.

But to this day, Churchill's visit to Madeira is fondly remembered.

and is found across the island) which were placed in the garden after being rescued from buildings that were being demolished.

Frederico de Freitas Museum

The Frederico de Freitas Museum on Calçada de Santa Clara is in part the legacy of a man to whom the museum owes its name: Frederico Augusto da Cunha Freitas. The museum, opposite the São Pedro parish church, is housed in the 18th-century former residence of this great collector who practised law in Madeira.

When it opened in 1988, the museum was an instant success. In particular because it houses a unique collection of decorative tiles from Turkish, Moorish/North African, and Hispano/Moorish origin. What started out as a hobby for the respected solicitor turned out to be a very impressive collection of Madeiran artefacts which started out with the proto-tile and continued to the late 1920s.

There are many fine art exhibits, too, including art by Portuguese and German artists, a wide variety of ceramic and porcelain pieces, religious sculptures, ancient sacred paintings, approximately 2000 mugs, trophies and vases, and a particularly fine collection of hand-carved metal and wooden sculptures of Chinese and North African origin.

Museum of Contemporary Art

The Museum of Contemporary Art opened in 1992 in the Fortaleza de São Tiago (Fort Saint James) in the Old Town of Funchal. Already it is regarded as one of the top five art museums in Portugal, boasting a collection of contemporary art donated by the artists themselves, and in that sense is unique.

The distinctive Portuguese and Madeiran art heritage is continuously expanding making it necessary to rotate the collection at intervals to accommodate all the works held by the museum. Significantly, the museum actively promotes the artists by allowing exhibitions of private collections during the year.

Among the regular artists are António Areal, Helena Almeida, Nuno Siqueira, Manuel Babtista, Jorge Martins, Artur Rosa, and Joaquim Rodrigo — all artists from the 60s. Artists from the 70s and 80s include Bartolomeu Cid dos Santos, Gil Teixeira Lopes, António Bouca, Cargaleiro, Emília Nadal, Carlos Calvet, António Palolo, Nuno Sampayo, Isabel Laginhas, and many others.

The most recent acquisitions have been works of art from the 90s including that of Ilda David, Ana Vidigal, Miguel Branco, Pedro Babrito Reis, Sofia Areal, Rui Sanches and António Campos Rosado.

Right: The Museum of Contemporary Art is housed in the Fortaleza de São Tiago (Fort Saint James) in the Old Town of Funchal, and regarded as among the finest art museums in Portugal.

Casa das Mudas Art Centre, Calheta

Madeira's largest cultural venue and the third largest in Portugal is not located in Funchal, but in Calheta about half an hour's drive away. Its aim is to provide a venue for art outside the cramped confines of the city, in a setting where 'lush mountainsides tumble down to the immensity of the ocean', and to raise public awareness of modern art and the arts in general. Opened in October 2004, the Centre was built as an extension of the old Casa das Mudas manor house. The inaugural exhibition

Above: 'Carnival' is celebrated across the whole island, and is a lavish manifestation of Brazilian-style revelry and good humour with numerous floats, bands, dancing and people in costume. Exciting, vibrant and hugely popular.

featured works by Picasso, Francis Bacon, Dali, Botero and Calder. Today it is also showing the work of some of the world's finest film-makers, including work by Stanley Kubrick.

Celebrations

The Madeiran year is filled with festivities, from official parades – usually for the benefit of visitors – to numerous local village and parish celebrations commemorating some event of distant, or even pagan significance.

Carnival

Ash Wednesday arrives in Madeira in the aftermath of days of carnival with the highlight coming in the form of the Cortejo Trapalhão, the costume parade, when, it seems, anything goes. On Friday of the week before,

Public Holidays and Festivals

Festivals can occur any time; the Madeiran people love to use any excuse for a party. But there are some regular public holidays and festivals that can affect your plans, as they invariably mean crowded roads, bars and restaurants.

1 January	New Year's Day	August, last Sunday	A carnival procession starts from
February	Carnival, celebrated across the island,		Machico, and ends with a huge bonfire
	and a spectacular affair involving lots		on Pico de Facho.
	of Brazilian-style revelry, with floats,	September	Apple Festival (Porto do Pargo and
	bands, dancers and people in		Camacha)
	stunning costumes.	September	Wine Festival (Estreito da Câmara de
March	Shrove Tuesday and Ash Wednesday		Lobos, Funchal and Porto da Cruz)
	Easter (dates vary)	September	Columbus week, a week long period of
25 April	Three-day Flower Festival (Funchal)		festivities on Porto Santo
	Day of the Revolution	5 October	Republic Day
1 May	Labour Day	1 November	All Saints' Day
June	Corpus Christi (dates vary)	November	Chestnut Festival (Festa das Castanhas),
10 June	National Day		folk displays and celebration of the
13 June	St Anthony's Day; the patron saint of		chestnut harvest in Curral das Freiras
	lovers – evening festivities include	1 December	Restoration of Independence Day
	leaping over fires	8 December	Immaculate Conception
24 June	St John's Day; the main saint's day	25/26 December	Christmas
	in Funchal	31 December	Annual firework display in Funchal; at
29 June	St Peter's Day; the patron saint of		midnight each New Year's Eve the bay
	fishermen, enthusiastically celebrated		becomes a fabulous extravaganza of
	in Câmara de Lobos and Ribeira Brava		fireworks. The display that saw in the
June	Vintage car rally, when some 60+		New Year of 2007 was officially
	vintage cars tour the island		declared and certified by the *Guinness*
	(dates vary)		*Book of Records* as the largest
1 July	National Day (Madeira Day)		pyrotechnics show in the world. Be
15 August	Feast of the Assumption: island-wide		aware that many hotels in Funchal
	celebrations with the biggest being		have very expensive and obligatory
	at Monte.		New Year's Eve 'Gala Dinners'; check
21 August	Funchal Day		before booking at this period.

Funchal is aroused by the sound of bands, people dancing and carnival parades that spread good humour across the whole city, but with the focus very much on the principal square, the Praça do Municipio. For five days running, the city celebrates. Saturday night is the time of the grand float parade, a gradual build up to the explosion of joy that is Shrove Tuesday.

Flower Festival

To understand why the people of Madeira are so enthusiastic about the Flower Festival, on the second Sunday after Easter, it is necessary to go back three decades when, in the aftermath of the 1974 'Carnation Revolution', Portugal went through a period of economic stagnation and more or less turned its back on the rest of Europe. This time coincided with Madeira's steps towards autonomy, and a time when the island was starting to make its presence felt as an international tourist destination.

The first Festa da Flor was held in 1979, and now, each year, the streets of Funchal are ablaze with floral colour as a Grand Parade passes through the city. Not only is the festival a celebration of all things bright and beautiful, but it is imbued with its own form of symbolism: the 'Wall of Hope', assembled in Largo do Municipio, is composed from thousands of flowers, and represents a wall of peace in stark contrast to the former Berlin Wall that for so long was the physical manifestation of the Cold War being played out in mainland Europe. Today, the Wall of Hope is a reminder of the many conflicts raging around the world, a spectacle that is as simple and naïve as it is beautiful, as hundreds of children place a flower onto a sea of flowers to build a wall of peace and hope.

This is a perfect time to visit the Flower Exhibition in Largo da Restauração, when unique species of orchid, anthurium and roses are on display.

Previous page: The New Year's Eve firework display is awesome and magnificent, a huge wave of pyrotechnics that embraces Funchal.
Left: The Flower Festival in April is a celebration of the island's floral wealth, and is popular with young and old alike.

Island Getaways

Left: This superb view of central Funchal is taken from the Quinta Bela São Tiago, one of the finest hotels in the 'Old Town'.

Ocean waves have for countless millions of years carved works of art from island coastlines, and Madeira is just as much a work of Nature's art. There is scarcely a kilometre of coastline that might be described as unattractive, even the busy bay of Funchal has appeal, especially at night when cruise ships are in port. Anyone wanting to get a true feeling for life on Madeira should take a couple of days to drive around the coastline, stopping off in tiny villages that cling to the edge of the island or to take photographs of the majestic scenery.

The most endearing inland beauty spots – Paúl da Serra, Boca da Encumeada, Curral das Freiras – are all easily reached by car (or taxi) from Funchal. Or you can put to sea, take a boat trip on catamarans or a replica of Christopher Columbus's ship the Santa Maria, to go whale or dolphin watching, or just to cruise along the coastline from Cabo Girão to the undulating peninsula of Ponta de São Lourenço.

Left: Stunning entrance of the Royal Savoy Hotel in Funchal.

Accommodation

There is no shortage of accommodation on Madeira; moreover, much of it is at the highest level of luxury. Four- and five-star hotels abound (indeed they are virtually the norm), quaint and botanically beautiful rural retreats (quintas) where attention to detail and a friendly welcome is all-important, ancient inns and hotels (estalagens), bright, modern hotels, spa resorts, and now the latest phenomenon, luxury apartment villas. Rates, other than at the best hotels in Funchal and at peak periods, are very reasonable. Hotel prices are directly affected by the demands of the tour operators, who want rooms at very low rates; this in turn influences the rates that can be charged away from Funchal. So it is always worth comparing rates at more than one hotel, and considering staying outside Funchal.

In recent years the island of Madeira has experienced a surge of development at many levels, not least the improvements to the infrastructure across the island, serving in the first instance to overcome the time taken to travel between Madeira's main towns. This development has also heralded an important change to the tourism scene, enabling discovery of the hinterland which until now has remained hidden from view beyond a tangle of badly maintained roads and excruciating

Hotels Galore!

In the interest of fairly representing high quality hotels across the island, rather than just in Funchal, some 'big hitters' are conspicuous in their absence – Reid's, for example – but those that are given have all been inspected and give a true picture of the ever-expanding range of superb accommodation on the island.

All the hotels listed here have their own dedicated website, but some feature as part of all-embracing websites, like www.quintas-madeira.com or www.charming hotelsmadeira.com, which give you access to a wider choice of hotels.

For comprehensive reviews of many of Madeira's hotels, consult www.hotelreviewmadeira.com

terrain. Rural tourism simply wasn't a concept to be entertained. But, with new roads, tunnels, bridges and better communications, rural tourism is adding a beautiful new dimension to the qualities of an already magnificent destination.

The grading system used for hotels on Madeira is generally accurate, and all three-, four- and five-star hotels offer air conditioning, television, direct dial telephone (but check the rates before using telephones, as these can be excessive), a garage and/or parking facilities, a restaurant and a bar. Of course, the star rating system is no real guarantee of setting, location, character, or quality of service.

Ever since Reid's opened in Funchal in the 19th century, Madeira has borne a well-earned reputation for quality accommodation and service, although some of the older hotels are beginning to show their age.

Left: Bedroom in Quinta Jardins do Lago; all the quintas are luxurious, elegant, sumptuous and dedicated to refined living and quality. Attention to detail is paramount, and the service impeccable. The Quinta Jardins do Lago is also justly proud of its superb restaurant serving traditional cuisine with inspiration.

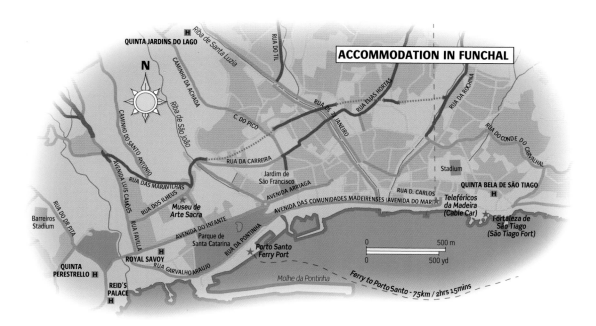

ACCOMMODATION IN FUNCHAL

Many of the hotels are in the so-called Hotel Zone at the western end of town, but there are many more both outside this zone – in the Old Town and high on the mountain slopes – and across wider Madeira, offering tranquil retreats and a relaxed atmosphere.

Usually privately owned, quintas offer the lifestyle of another age, one of refinement, utmost quality and luxury, the elegance of palaces, and often surrounded by beautiful gardens and lakes. These are the homes of former aristocratic families, places where fragments of other lifetimes and the history of old Madeira are embedded in their culture, the mansions and grand houses of another era, but with a very modern emphasis on luxury and good taste. Many also have excellent restaurants, leaving the visitor with little to do but chill out and be pampered. Quintas are islands within an island, and very much for the quietly discerning traveller, with or without a family in tow. The 'Quintas da Madeira' is a new tourism scheme available to visitors who prefer smaller hotels in quiet locations, and currently includes 16 hotels in various parts of the island.

Each quinta hotel meets at least seven of the nine criteria required to become part of the scheme. These embrace the existence of the original house, which needs to be carefully and tastefully blended with modern extensions; special attention has to be paid to luxury, comfort, modern conveniences, historical background, four- or five-star rating, and no more than 70 rooms. They must also possess gardens with mature trees, native species and ornamental landscaping that blends with the natural surroundings, and have a ratio of 30% buildings to 70% gardens. What all this adds up to is luxury in superb surroundings.

Medieval hostelries – estalagens – owned, like quintas, by individuals or maintained by the property owners themselves, have rules of propriety established by royal decree since 10 February 1269, when the king himself signed the creation letter for the Estalagem de Coimbra in Portugal. The keepers of estalagens were traditionally obliged to offer clothing and anything else travellers might need for themselves or their horses. Throughout the 15th century such hostelries spread rapidly through-

out mainland Portugal, so it was only a matter of time before the services these ancient inns offered found a renaissance as Madeira's tourist trade slowly began.

In time, Funchal saw the creation of many hotels, but if using Funchal as a base made sense in the early days of tourism, given the dearth of accommodation alternatives elsewhere, that is no longer the case, and the choice of places to stay has expanded across the entire island. Indeed many of today's visitors choose to stay at hotels away from the bustle of central Funchal. Self-catering apartments and country hotels are widely spread, and now there is the rising star of holiday villa complexes, a translocation of ideas from mainland Portugal, but one that is offering the discerning traveller and those who cherish the isolation and tranquillity of independent holidays another dimension into which to retreat.

Funchal
Quinta Jardins do Lago ★★★★★

Located on one of the hills above Funchal and overlooking the sea, this charming Madeiran family home was built in the 1750s, and most recently was the home of French and British families, notably General Beresford, commander of the British forces at the time of the Napoleonic wars. His magnificent sideboard still adorns the restaurant. The gardens, proudly supervised by the hotel's part-owner and Managing Director, are unique in

Previous page: The swimming pool area at the Quinta Jardins do Lago is typical of those you find at all the major hotels across Madeira. Emphasis is on refined relaxation where everything is provided and nothing left to chance. Enclosed in a walled garden, the Quinta Jardins do Lago is skillfully designed for relaxation.
Right: 'Savoy' – a byword for luxury, and the Royal Savoy on Madeira is no exception. The Savoy Resort is the swishiest place in town, arranged above a series of palm-fringed seafront pools, bars and restaurants, with its own sea access. There are two 'Savoy' hotels, the one offering modern styling and décor, the other all the period elegance and refinement associated with Savoy hotels.

their variety, containing many rare species of flowers, shrubs and ancient trees from many parts of the world.

All 31 spacious bedrooms, five suites and four junior suites have south-facing living rooms and balconies overlooking the gardens. The interior of the main house has been refurbished to its original standard and offers a refinement in keeping with its roots. It is an eminently successful blending of elegance, history and comfort.

The Beresford Restaurant, with al fresco seating for balmy evenings, offers Madeiran and international cuisine served to the highest standards and with keen attention to detail. The Pink Room, with a view over the gardens, indeed actually in the gardens if you wish, has a splendid 16th-century ceramic wall panel, and is the place to take breakfast.

O Visconde is a cosy bar in the main lounge, ideal for pre-dinner drinks, cocktails, after-dinner dancing and relaxing to the sound of live music. The Colombo Bistro, found near the semi-covered swimming pool offers drinks, snacks and quality food prepared from fresh local ingredients. It is named after a giant Galapagos tortoise that lives in the grounds of the hotel.

You can relax on the sunbeds, in the sauna, the Turkish bath or the Jacuzzi, or you can head for the tennis courts or a workout in the gym. There is also free Internet access (communal).

Hotel Royal Savoy ★★★★★

Throughout the world 'Savoy' is a byword for luxury, for pampering, for all the good things in hotel accommodation. The Savoy on Madeira is no exception, but, just to be on the safe side, there are two of them – the Classic Savoy and the Royal Savoy.

The Savoy Resort is just about the swishiest place in town, from which it is only a few minutes' walk. Overlooking the beautiful Funchal Bay the Savoy Resort offers 325 spacious rooms and 12 sea view suites all with individual balcony and ocean or mountain views. The Royal Savoy is arranged above a series of palm-fringed seafront pools, bars and restaurants, with its own sea access, while the Classic Savoy sits a little

higher, and is linked to the newer hotel by a private bridge. By means of this bridge, guests at either hotel may enjoy all the facilities of both. In the Royal, glass-sided lifts whisk you to all levels in search of the spa, bars and restaurants.

The Classic Savoy is one of Funchal's oldest hotels, and it displays a period elegance that would be out of place in the brash youngster next door – not that 'brash' could ever be a truly appropriate word for a Savoy Hotel.

Between the two there is a vast array of facilities, from spas, a gymnasium, beauty treatment rooms and golf practice nets to a fine range of restaurants serving high quality Madeiran and traditional European cuisine. The Fleur de Lys Restaurant, on the eighth floor of the Classic Savoy, serves excellent international cuisine, but the staff are a little over-attentive, and gentlemen need to wear a tie.

Quinta Bela São Tiago ★★★★★

Found in the old and rather quieter part of Funchal, the Quinta Bela São Tiago has a panoramic view over the harbour, ideal for the summertime and New Year firework displays. Built in 1894 in the colonial style by a Madeiran family, the house was, until 1910, the private residence of Madeira's Deputy Governor.

Here in the Old Town, the cobbled streets, a web of small and narrow streets, are a maze in themselves and a delight to wander. The tiny houses are painted with bright colours, and many have been converted into bars and restaurants. Some of the oldest streets in Madeira are found here, many dating from the very early 16th century, and the Quinta Bela São Tiago a perfect base from which to explore.

The house was restored and extended in 1998 in keeping with its architectural pedigree, and today offers 64 luxurious guest rooms including two junior

Right: The Quinta Bela São Tiago is built in an elevated position, in the old part of Funchal, and boasts panoramic views over the sea, the mountains and the bay of Funchal. Initially built in 1894 in colonial style for a traditional Madeiran family, until the beginning of the 20th century, this house was the residence of Madeira's Deputy Governor.

suites, three de luxe suites, one executive de luxe suite, a Presidential Suite and a Penthouse Suite. All the rooms are air conditioned and supplied with telephone, cable television and Internet connection, minibar and sumptuous bathrooms. Elsewhere the hotel offers private parking, an outdoor heated pool, Jacuzzi, Turkish bath, sauna, gymnasium, and its very own banana plantation.

The 'O Portico' restaurant, in the old part of the house, serves regional and international cuisine in refined surroundings, or on the Governor's Terrace with a fine seaward view. The terrace is a perfect place to take an early breakfast and watch the sun rise. And, at the end of the day, the Por do Sol Cocktail Bar is perfect for an after-dinner malmsey.

Quinta Bela Vista ★★★★★

Occupied by the Ornelas Monteiro family since its construction in 1844, the Quinta Bela Vista is dedicated to making you feel comfortable in luxurious surroundings. The Quinta is set in old, established gardens featuring trees and plants from many parts of the world like kapok, paulownia and hibiscus, and with narrow, cobbled pathways. For antique lovers, Bela Vista is some kind of Heaven on earth; the owner is an avid and talented antique collector and his outstanding private collection of mainly English furniture from the 16th to 18th centuries adorns every room in the hotel. But the key thing about Bela Vista is that you don't have the impression of being in a hotel, but rather in a sumptuous house as a personal guest of the owner.

Left: The interior of the Quinta Bela Vista is a cornucopia of antiques, many of them rare and of historical importance. For lovers of antiques and antiquity, this remarkable and refined hotel is some kind of heaven on earth.
Right: The Quinta do Monte, set high above Funchal in the village of Monte is perfectly placed for visits to the Monte Palace Garden, the Madeira Botanical Garden and the traditional toboggan run, which starts from just below the hotel.

Located on the outskirts of Funchal, five minutes from the centre, the hotel is certainly very quiet, and many of the 89 guestrooms have views either of the mountains or the Funchal bay, ideal, in fact, from which to watch firework displays. There are seven luxurious suites that have in their time accommodated royalty, and four guest rooms suitably adapted for wheelchair guests.

An à la carte menu of Madeiran/European fusion dishes is available in the Casa Mãe, the original house, while the nearby Avista Navios offers a table d'hôte menu.

Without doubt, the Quinta Bela Vista, having consistently won awards for its service, is one of the most select and exclusive family properties on Madeira, an outstanding place in which to relax, unwind, or be romantic.

Quinta Perestrello ★★★★

It is easy to forget in the comforting surroundings of the 150-year-old Quinta Perestrello that the pulsating heart of Funchal is only a 10-minute walk away. Set in the most prestigious hotel area, Perestrello reflects the traditional décor of Madeira's heritage, and is larger than it looks, offering 37 rooms, all with wooden floors, air conditioning, cable television and double glazing.

Rooms in the modern extension have their own terraces.

A small, but adequate outdoor swimming pool is a perfect place to relax at the end of the day, before a dinner of Madeiran and international cuisine in the hotel restaurant.

Quinta do Monte ★★★★★

Perched high on the slopes above Funchal, in the tiny, picturesque community of Monte, the Quinta do Monte

Below: The view from the Calheta Beach Hotel; the beaches at Calheta are the only golden sand beaches on Madeira, and are man-made with sand imported from mainland Portugal and Morocco. The pedigree of the sand, however, detracts not at all from the popularity of this and the adjacent beach.

is a dream location. Also known as the Quinta Cossart, after the Englishman who formerly lived here, the Monte was also the sometime residence of Charles, the last Emperor of Austria. It is reached by a dramatic winding road that seems never to end and is eminently suitable for anyone wanting to be away from it all, in a setting of calm and peacefulness. Once installed, access to Funchal is made easy by a cable car, or, for the adventurous, the dry toboggan run, which starts nearby and takes you half way to Funchal – you complete the trip by taxi.

The Quinta is surrounded by a huge garden of lush vegetation that wraps the hotel in a comforting silence. Its 42 rooms all have air conditioning, telephone, satellite television and minibar. A splendid restaurant serving international cuisine and Madeiran specialities

is complemented by free Internet connection (communal), a bar, tea room, a heated indoor swimming pool set apart from the hotel, gymnasium, Jacuzzi and Turkish bath.

Estreito da Câmara de Lobos
Quinta Estreito

Found among the vineyards on the southern slopes of the main wine producing area of Madeira, situated just below the village of Estreito, the Quinta Estreito was formerly the main wine producing estate in the area. Today, the original house, built in 1914 for the family of Vega França, has been carefully restored to become the Bacchus Gourmet Restaurant, bar and library reading room, with stunning views down to the sea.

The décor of the reception and public areas reflects a bygone elegance and luxury. The guest rooms all face south and are decorated in beige and cream with light oak wooden floors, and marble and oak bathrooms. All rooms have a balcony with a sea view, air conditioning, cable television and telephone. There are superb views of the surrounding hills, the southern coast of the island, and the shimmering Atlantic Ocean. A sauna and solarium complete the hotel's charms, which extend to complimentary use of the spa at the Quinta das Vistas in Funchal and of all the facilities at other hotels in the Charming Hotels network.

The beautifully tended gardens include a small olive grove, a formal French garden, a range of tropical plants and the heavily Madeiran dining experience that is the Adega da Quinta Restaurant.

Above: *Tucked away on the edge of the laurissilva forest and close to popular levadas, Átrio is a real find, and a luxurious mini-hotel away from the crowds of Funchal. This tranquil retreat is popular with walkers and those who want a quiet time during their stay on Madeira.*

Calheta

Hotel Calheta Beach ★★★★

About 45 minutes from Funchal, the Calheta Beach Hotel is immediately adjacent the resort's imported beach, composed of sand brought from Morocco and mainland Portugal. It's a neat idea, and works very well, especially on a volcanic island where golden beaches are virtually non-existent.

The Calheta Beach Hotel is a modern building, but one that makes your money go further as even the most expensive rooms are significantly cheaper than comparable rooms in Funchal ... and the modest resort of Calheta has most things you might need.

As for the hotel, there are 89 standard rooms, four junior suites, one master suite, and 10 apartments in an adjacent building. Most of the rooms have a sea view, but if you want to be sure of one, check on booking. Two restaurants serving Madeiran and international dishes, two bars, an outdoor swimming pool, an indoor heated pool, sauna and steam bath are all added attractions, with the golden sands just a few strides away. And, by arrangement, you can enjoy a range of beauty treatments, massages and Thalasso treatments, or simply work off lunch in the gymnasium. Unlike some of the central hotels, the Calheta Beach is very much family oriented.

Átrio

Unlikely, for the moment, to feature in many of the glossy brochures, Átrio is a real find – an island of calm on an island of tranquillity. Built by a German mountain guide and French yoga instructress, Átrio, essentially a

European-style country inn, sits at the very edge of the central forest of Madeira and offers proximity to nature and personal service.

It is easy to find, but when you go there for the first time you'll probably still need to take a taxi. This delightful 10-roomed establishment is furnished very much in its own idiosyncratic style, with lovely bedrooms, some with balconies, others facing out onto the garden and terrace. It is the product of the wave of development that has facilitated an expansion of rural tourism, and an ideal platform from which to discover the island's natural heritage.

A small, heated, outdoor swimming pool is a perfect place to relax after a day tramping along the nearby Levada da Calheta, while the tumbling, flower-filled garden is perfect for an after-dinner drink.

Átrio offers the best of two worlds: energetic levada walking, and end-of-day relaxation. What could be better?

Porto Moniz
Hotel Moniz Sol ★★★

This modest hotel is located near the aquarium overlooking the northern coastline of Madeira. There are 42 balconied rooms with sea view, and six with mountain

Below: The Estalagem do Mar caters very purposefully for visitors to the north coast of the island. On the edge of São Vicente, the hotel boasts all modern conveniences and faces out to the sea. São Vicente and the north coast is the place to come to get as close as you can to the 'real' way of life in Madeira. Vines and orchards dot the hillsides, farmed by traditional methods.

view, plus one suite. Direct telephone is available in all rooms along with cable television, air conditioning and security provision.

São Vicente
Estalagem do Mar ★★★★

This four-star hotel located on the beach near Sao Vicente village is an agreeable alternative to the city, on the north coast of Madeira island, 40km (25 miles) from the capital city Funchal, and 60km (37 miles) from the airport. All 91 rooms and eight junior suites have sea view, twin or double beds, private bathroom, television, direct-dial

Previous page: Quinta Splendida in the village of Caniço is virtually a destination in itself. Modern and spacious in concept and design the emphasis here is on gourmet cuisine and wellbeing. A new 'Wellness' area, tapping into the tourist theme of pampering and luxury spa treatments, offers everything for those who want to escape the pressures of modern life and to revitalize.

phone, hairdryer, safe box for hire, wicker chairs and table, light beige decor with dark rose carpet, flowery curtains and dark wooden furniture. The hotel offers a tennis court, gym, billiards and snooker, games room with table tennis and darts, sauna, Jacuzzi, heated indoor pool, outdoor pool, WiFi connection in lobby (fee), large garden with loungers, gallery bar and occasional entertainment.

The hotel offers a 24-hour reception, a meeting room, car parking, mailing service, doctor/clinic (24 hours) two min. drive, baby-sitting upon request, luggage storage, foreign currency exchange, and car rental.

Santana
Hotel O Colmo ★★★★

For those who prefer to avoid the bustle of Funchal, Santana, a quiet unassuming village famed for its A-framed houses, is perfect, and the Hotel O Colmo very much so. This modern, family-run enterprise, around 20 minutes from the airport, has 40 rooms and three suites, with balconies, garden view, telephone, satellite tele-

vision and central heating. All rooms are brightly decorated and boast everything you might expect from a quality four-star rural hotel. For a little relaxation there's an indoor heated pool, Jacuzzi, sauna, Turkish bath and a small gymnasium. But what makes the hotel just that extra bit special is its outstanding restaurant (*see* page 155); when you see locals coming in for lunch, you know there has to be something good.

Caniço
Hotel Quinta Splendida ★★★★★

Situated on the boundary between the two long-established districts of Funchal and Machico, the village of Caniço is the site of the first sugar mill on the island. The manor house, which forms the core of the Quinta Splendida, was built in the 18th century, and was a property of Jesuit priests; the old name of the house was Quinta Estrela.

In the mid-19th century, Quinta Estrela was bought by Fortunato Joaquim Figueira, baron of Conceição, who

Above: The Quinta Serra Golfe, as its name suggests, is closely allied with the nearby 27-hole golf course, one of international standing. The hotel is modest in proportion, but set in a relatively remote part of the island, although just 15 minutes from the airport, offers an 'away-from-it-all' atmosphere and uncomplicated dining experiences. It is quite simply peaceful and refreshing.

made his fortune in the wine trade, and began planting the botanical garden for which today's hotel is renowned. In 1989, the present owner effected major changes, clearing large areas of land and restoring the manor house. Four years later, the refurbished hotel was opened under the name Hotel Quinta Splendida, and is commonly regarded as one of the most beautiful hotels in Madeira.

The hotel has 141 guestrooms, all of them sumptuously furnished and decorated; 28 units with either garden or sea views were added in 1999, and a further 25 luxurious and spacious suites in contemporary design were completed in 2006. The gourmet restaurant La Perla and five

rooms are located in the manor house. Two more restaurants support La Perla: La Galeria serves Mediterranean dishes in a traditional setting, while the Thai Lounge offers Thai and Asian fusion cuisine (*see* Island Cuisine).

In addition, Splendida has a new 'Wellness' area, described as a sanctuary to escape the pressures of modern life. This superb spa facility features a vitality pool, and indoor pool and 10 rooms for a variety of treatments, including a double massage room for couples, cardiovascular suite, traditional sauna, Turkish steam bath and a mud bath. It is the largest and most comprehensive 'Wellness' complex in Madeira.

With so much on offer you would expect Splendida to feel crowded, but its thoughtful layout and design means that even when it is full there is no sense of other people intruding on your holiday. It is a masterpiece of planning. Thirty thousand square meters of botanical garden, featuring over 1000 plants and flowers does much to underscore the spaciousness of the Splendida, and the evident desire to make clients feel comfortable and relaxed. It succeeds, admirably.

Santo da Serra
Quinta Serra Golfe

Once a tea house and the clubhouse of the Clube de Golf Santo da Serra, Quinta Serra Golfe has long been the setting for social and cultural events. Encircled by the protected laurissilva forest, the hotel's main raison d'être, however, is to provide the best possible service for golfers (and non-golfers). It may be a 'golfers' hotel, but there is no evidence of that, just an agreeable ambience that is both relaxing and invigorating.

The building was completely renovated in 1920, having belonged to the same family since its construc-

Left: The attraction of Porto Santo's sandy beach makes it a popular destination for residents of Madeira and visitors alike. The Hotel Porto Santo is among the best of a growing number of accommodation providers on the island, and combines luxury and refinement with al fresco dining and a direct access to those golden sands.

tion. It is undoubtedly a hotel of distinction, hugely relaxing and in one of the quietest parts of the island. Eighteen twin rooms, two junior suites and one suite with a sitting room and kitchenette mean that the hotel never feels crowded. The restaurant offers simple and inexpensive dishes, and a modest wine list that will help relieve the stress of coping with the 27-hole golf course just a few minutes away.

Located just 15 minutes from the airport, and 30 minutes from Funchal, Quinta Serra Golfe offers a peaceful retreat for those who want to escape the energy of Funchal.

Eira do Serrado
Estalagem Eira do Serrado ★★★★

Superbly placed for a visit to the inner sanctum that is Curral das Freiras, this modern hotel offers 17 elegantly decorated rooms and eight superior rooms, each with a balcony overlooking the distant village, air conditioning and satellite television. There is also a sauna, Jacuzzi, games room, and a restaurant serving Madeiran dishes, many with a hint of chestnut, which grows profusely here.

Anyone looking for a calm retreat, away from the bustle of Funchal, will find it here – once the tour buses have departed for the day. There is an eyrie-like feeling about the place, although there are no eagles, and an eerie sensation when the mists rolls over the col from the valley to the south.

Porto Santo
Hotel Porto Santo ★★★★

This discreet, low-rise hotel is the most sophisticated on the island, set in a palm-studded garden with direct access to the beach. The rooms have all the facilities you would expect, including balconies, cable television and air conditioning. There is a fine restaurant, and a pool bar/brasserie for outdoor dining, and a small swimming pool with a separate children's pool. The hotel can arrange most activities including watersports, horse riding and bicycle hire.

Shopping and Markets

Left: *On the south side of Largo do Achada in Camacha is O Relógio, once the home of a British merchant's family, and today a huge, rambling souvenir shop with a vast range of wickerwork and local produce.*

Shopping until you drop is probably not one of the most important ingredients in a stay on Madeira, but if you wanted to, you could. Shopping centres, especially in Funchal, are plentiful, as are designer outlets, mainly for Portuguese goods. Beware of imported items from further afield as these are needlessly expensive.

Beyond the conventional shopping arcades, the Funchal market is a bazaar in the classic style, adjoined by a rather gruesome fish market. Elsewhere, shopping emporiums are few, although Camacha is the base for all things wickerwork. But keep an eye open for local people selling goods in the remote villages; you can often see them actually making the items. At least, that way you can be sure it's authentic.

With the exception of the Mercado dos Lavradores in Funchal, open markets mainly serve the local population, who do their weekly shopping there. Usually held at the weekends, these typical markets can be found everywhere on the island, but the more established ones are in Porto Moniz, Ponta Delgada and Santo da Serra.

Left: With so many flowers available on the island, it's not surprising to find flower markets everywhere. Taking flowers home as a souvenir is increasingly an important feature of the island economy.

Shopping in Madeira

Because the vast majority of Madeira's goods have to be imported, the best-value items are those produced locally, notably wickerwork, embroidery, tapestry and knitwear. Increasingly, orchid plants and seedlings are becoming part of the tourist's mementoes of the island, while conventional souvenirs range from excellent, skilfully made products to downright embarrassing and tacky. Madeira wine is, perhaps not surprisingly, the most popular buy, and, although you can find it for sale in most towns across the island, it is in Funchal that you'll find the adegas where you can taste before you buy. If it's Madeira wine you seek, then there are quite a few places that will put your palate to the test. The Vinhos Barbeito, behind Reid's Palace Hotel, is a long-established wine lodge; by comparison ABSL (which stands for Artur de Barros e Sousa Lda. – see page 34) on the Rue dos Ferreiros in Funchal is so tiny it is difficult to find, and the producers, two brothers, only sell to friends – but don't be deterred; as you pass through the door, you become a 'friend'. Anyone staying in the hotel district will find the late-opening Loja dos Vinhos on the Rua do Gorgulho a good place to find a last-minute vintage wine, including many that are over 100 years old. But if you want to combine a little history with a little atmosphere and perhaps a tasting or two, then the place to go is the Blandy family's enterprise, Adegas de São Francisco on the Avenida Arriaga in Funchal (near the tourist office). Amid vats and barrels and a heady atmosphere, you can wander freely through the buildings, alongside one of the oldest streets in Madeira, and sample wines for free in the Max Romer Tasting Bar decorated with murals of grape growing and harvesting. Or you can wait for one of the guided tours through what remains of the 16th-century friary around which the adega is built.

The main market in Funchal (Mercado dos Lavradores) is a wondrous bazaar to explore, and many of the fruit sellers will offer you some to taste before buying. A frenetic bustle of good humour, the market is a perfect place to shop for picnic ingredients, or just to see what is going on. Shopaholics will love the retail therapy offered by Madeira Shopping on Caminho de Santa Quitéria, Santo António; it's a short taxi ride (or if you're driving follow signs from the São Martinho exit on the expressway), but here you will find well over 100 shops, including many major European brands, plus 19 restaurants and seven cinemas, and free parking for over 1000 cars.

Funchal's most trendy and upmarket shopping mall is Galerias São Lourenço on Avenida Arriaga where you can buy anything from stylish sunglasses to refined tableware; you could probably find a pink elephant, too, if you looked closely enough. The Crosby Collection behind the cathedral on Rua da Sé and adjoining the café-laden Largo do Colombo (where you can take a post-shopping glass of malvasia), is the largest clothing store on Madeira, spread across an entire building and five floors, selling many top brands. Closer to the seafront, the Marina Shopping Centre is surprisingly compact and complex, and ranges from chic cafés and a splendid Chinese Restaurant (Fu Hao – see page 151) at ground level, to boutiques selling clothing, crafts, trinkets, souvenirs, books, postcards, maps, surfing gear, photographic supplies and pizzas. If you are hunting embroidery items, tapestry, leatherwork and souvenirs, take time to check out the Rua dos Murças, a narrow, city-centre street off Avenida Zarco, and full of shops where you can often find good bargains. But the main shopping street is the Rua Fernão Ornelas, a bizarre mix of chic boutiques, grocers, newsagents, coffee shops and fish shops. The Bazar do Povo is

Right: *The production of wine is an important element in the island's economy, and one of the features for which Madeira has long been renowned. Prince Henry 'the Navigator' is believed to have introduced the first vines to Madeira during the early period of colonization. Later, wine was made by Jesuit priests. But the greatest aid to the burgeoning wine industry was initiated by the British during the 18th century, from when wine was exported in quantities up to 20,000 barrels per year. These days, the island produces over 5 million bottles of Madeira wine annually.*

Funchal's oldest 'department store', the 'People's Bazaar', and sells everything from CDs and DVDs to souvenirs and religious memorabilia.

Wickerwork

Wickerwork has long been a small cottage industry in Madeira, serving local needs. Legend has it that this craft was brought back to Madeira in the 1850s by a prisoner serving his time in Lisbon, who then taught his villagers. But the industry didn't expand until a British

Above: Wickerwork has long been associated with Madeira, and is found all across the island. In Funchal, look along the Rua do Castanheiro. But the principal centre is Camacha, where around 2000 people are employed in making wickerwork products. Finding them, however, is no easy thing, for they tend to work in isolation in small workshops attached to houses.

sugar merchant, William Hinton, persuaded local farmers to diversify, and not to be so over-reliant on wine production. Long before Hinton, however, the distinctively cone-shaped barreleiros were used to transport fruit, rocks and soil about the terraces.

Following Hinton's intervention, a healthy appetite for wickerwork, especially cane furniture, soon evolved notably in the British colonies. For a time, production dropped, but then better production techniques and a more focused approach to manufacturing, marketing and the production of raw materials helped craftsmen to fabricate a much wider range of products, of all shapes and sizes.

Today, tourist demand keeps around 2000 people employed, mainly around Camacha, although you have to scour the back streets to find any of them. Thankfully, the south side of Largo do Achada in Camacha is where you'll find O Relógio, once the home of a British merchant's family, and today a huge and rambling souvenir shop with a vast range of wicker products (and some really tacky souvenirs). You may think that there are only so many things you can do with wicker, but a visit to O Relógio will persuade you otherwise.

Wicker is produced from willows, and these thrive in the damp ground around Camacha, but are increasingly transported from the equally damp ground along the north coast, notably around Boaventura. The larger branches are used like conventional wood, but the more flexible branches are gathered in spring, soaked, stripped of their bark and dried to form wicker.

Embroidery

Some of the oldest surviving examples of embroidery (bordados) – rich 16th- and 17th-century vestments – were created by the nuns in the Convent of Santa Clara in Funchal, and are now on display in the Museum of Sacred Art. The art arrived on Madeira with the early settlers, and, at the time, was exclusively the domain of noblewomen. But it was the work of an Englishwoman, Elizabeth Phelps, the daughter of a wine merchant, that initiated the cottage industry in embroidery and brought its quality and diversity to the attention of the wider world. Phelps' charity work for a local orphanage in Santana, included teaching children how to embroider,

Flowery Souvenirs

Madeiran flowers – Cymbidium orchid, bird of paradise, king protea, magnolia, flamingo flowers – are an increasingly popular souvenir to take home; if nothing else it helps to make the holiday last a while longer. Flowers can be purchased anywhere in Funchal, at the local market, the flower stands in the city centre, in the flower shops or in some of the botanical gardens. In all these places your flowers will be packed in special boxes for safe transport. But be sure to declare them at the airport as your depart, and quite possibly on arrival at your home airport, too.

and her fascination with the intricate skills and designs persuaded her to take samples to the Great Exhibition in London in 1851, where they caused a huge sensation among the ladies of the Victorian Court. Suddenly, Madeira embroidery acquired a vogue, and the choice of young brides in high society. Before long demand far exceeded supply until a firm was established in 1862 to give the enterprise a formal commercial base. More than 1000 jobs were soon created, a timely event as many men were still seeking work following a disaster in the vineyards, and now their wives were able to produce a much-needed income. But there was more to come.

Around 1900, the demand for hand-crafted embroidery was waning. But then a German mogul, targeting the American and German markets, devised a technique that enabled the designs to be printed directly onto the fabric rather than time-consuming pre-stitching. This revolutionized the industry, gave it the boost it needed, and by the 1920s, around 70,000 women were employed making embroidery items.

Today, the number is around one-tenth of that, but embroidery remains an industry that rivals wine export. Crochet and knitwear is also popular and makes ideal souvenirs. Usually the bordadeiras (seamstresses) work from home, with whole generations of families acquiring and passing on the skills. But it is not unusual to

find them working at retail outlets; this is particularly fascinating because when you actually see them working you realize that many of the items are the product of a team rather than an individual. Two or three women often work on the same piece, each specializing in a particular stitch or design feature. Afterwards, the embroidery is taken to 'factories' in Funchal or Machico for final stitching where it is washed and ironed before receiving the seal of authenticity from IBTAM (*see* page 79). Most

Left: The exquisite artwork of embroidery is a delight. Available through many retail outlets, it is also possible to buy embroidery locally across the island from the hands of those who actually make it.

Following page: *Remote villages like Curral das Freiras are an ideal place to find traditional goods being made and sold, often at much lower prices than you might pay in Funchal shops, although there is no real need to haggle – prices are remarkably reasonable given the skill and time involved in production.*

embroidery is packaged for the export market, or sold on to shops in and around Funchal. Sadly, the number of stages in the production process has an impact on price, making the best items very expensive. Alas, only a small proportion finds its way back to the person who did the stitching.

The main export markets are Britain, France, Germany and Italy, but today there is aggressive competition from the Far East, where labour costs are lower; that seal of authenticity is the key to buying the pukka product and not some cheap import. Tapestry was a later introduction to the island, but cannot compete with the enthusiasm for embroidery.

The hand embroidery of Madeira is widely recognized as the finest of its kind in the world. Over the last 150 years, Madeira has embraced expertise from the fast-disappearing centres of hand embroidery across Europe and transformed the many individual styles into a unique Madeiran package, that in terms of quality is unsurpassed.

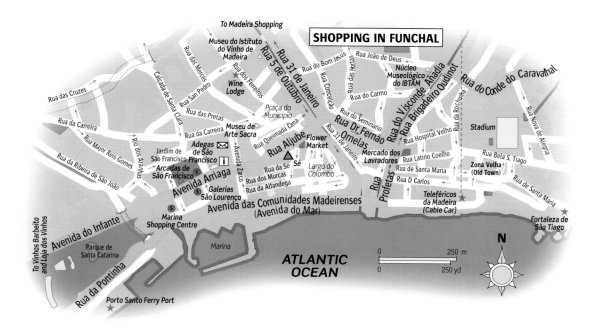

Knitwear

Keep an eye open for local people making barrettes de lã, the ear-flapped pom-pom hats that are a customary part of male Madeiran farmer's attire. They are excellent protection against cold winds, and come in sober brown, or gaudy, kaleidoscopic colours. The best bargains are not found in souvenir shops, which treat them as novelty items and charge accordingly. You can get them much more cheaply from craft shops, or even from vendors in the streets.

Footwear

The traditional, rather odd-looking ankle boots, often soled with car tyres (as used by the men who steer the toboggans at Monte), are very strong and long lasting, and you can get them at many shops in Funchal, as well as a fine line in handmade shoes. As with most things, go to shoe shops rather than souvenir shops for this kind of memento.

Markets and Supermarkets

The renowned market in the old part of Funchal town is essential visiting; this is not just a market, it's an institution, and a lively one at that. Here is a good place to see and sample first-hand the colourful fruits, and begin

Below: One popular souvenir of Madeira is the traditional hat worn in folkloric displays and dances. In countless design and colours the hats are a round knit or woven toque with a flat top and embroidered edges. On the top is a tail, often with a pom-pom. They are fairly inexpensive and easy to carry: very Madeiran, colourful and fun, and, who knows, something to keep you warm in bed on a cold winter's night!

learning something about Madeira's beautiful flowers. Mingle with the locals, eavesdrop, taste, prod, smell, chinwag and buy. The atmosphere is buzzing, and the market stall holders more than willing to help you.

On the evening of the 23rd of December everyone visits the market; all the stalls are open until well after midnight, and you can buy last minute presents and food to get you through the Christmas period. There is a wonderful atmosphere, not surprising then that this tradition has lasted for so long.

There are a number of good supermarkets around Funchal selling Portuguese and an increasing number of international products – and with fresh fruit and vegetables always available. The main supermarket chains are SA and Pingo Doce. Elsewhere, in each part of Madeira there are small local stores where you will find most products.

Some Shopping Tips

• Don't assume, as is often the case, that you can necessarily get bargains at the Duty Free shop at the airport; you may, but you are just as likely, if not more so, to find that things are in many cases cheaper in the wine shops and supermarkets in Funchal.

• Steer clear of leather products in general; prices on Madeira are invariably higher than elsewhere in Europe because of the cost of importing items. The exception are shoes, which are Portuguese specialities, and you'll find plenty of shops in the streets around the cathedral. Of course, if you're not going to mainland Europe, and there is something you really, really like ...

• Embroidery, crochet work, knitting and tapestry produced on Madeira is checked for quality and usually has a tag or seal to signify that it is genuine. Beware of high-priced, machine-made embroidery imported from Asia. This is one occasion when a visit to the quality shops in Funchal is justified to be sure you get the quality product. Some of the souvenir knitwear – hats, shawls and cardigans – carries no identification. You need to let yourself be persuaded that it is genuine. Often you can see women working on items while waiting to serve people – Encumeada and Curral das Freitas are places in point – and as you watch their dizzy fingerwork you can be tolerably certain that this is the real thing! There is simply no point fuelling a distant economy when that on Madeira needs all the help it can get.

• If you want to take flowers back, try to get them delivered to your hotel on the morning of your departure. They should be packed in strong and sterile cardboard containers, and the island's florists are quite aware of what they need to do. Protea and orchids are particularly well suited to air travel! – but don't buy them too far ahead of your return.

• If you really want a souvenir of Madeira, buy some honey cake (bolo de Mel); this dense and fruity cake is available all year round and is easily packed. Unfortunately, while it keeps very well for quite a few months, it doesn't last very long once you get it home – no matter how well-intentioned you are.

Island Cuisine

Left: *The abundance of fresh fruit and vegetables on Madeira is nowhere better seen than at the Mercado dos Lavradores in Funchal.*

Madeira's cuisine makes the most of
what is readily available – seafood, fruit and
vegetables. Yet even with this limited palette,
the island's chefs are proving more than
adept at culinary improvisation and innovation.
In the main, the island's cuisine follows
long-established traditions, but there is an
increasing move to modern interpretations
of those traditions. It all makes for enjoyable
dining, whether in the top restaurants and
hotels or in 'back street' restaurants. There is,
too, an increasing move towards Pan-European
and Asian food.

*Left: Seafood dish in the restaurant
at the Quinta da Bela Vista.*

Madeiran Cuisine

Madeiran cuisine is much inspired by the island's agriculture and setting; the rich soil and superb climate make the fruit and vegetables grow quickly and with intense flavour.

The seas surrounding Madeira are abundantly rich in marine life, so it is not surprising that fish, in one form or another, features large in the island's culinary repertoire, although the principal influence is Mediterranean, using garlic and imported olive oil. Ironically, scabbard fish (espada), so called because it resembles a sword, one of the ugliest fish, dredged from the depths of the sea, takes centre stage on many menus. Despite its fiercesome appearance – take a visit to the Funchal fish market to see for yourself – this long, wide-eyed, sharp-toothed fish produces a delicious boneless, white flesh which the Madeiran chefs often serve with banana or in a wine and vinegar marinade.

Other fish dishes are tuna (atum), usually served grilled as a steak with lemon, grouper (garopa), red mullet (salmonete – not to be confused with salmon, which is salmão), salt cod (bacalhau), sea bass (cheme), sea bream (pargo), trout (truta), parrot fish (bodião) and swordfish (espadarte). Grilled mackerel with onion and spice sauce (Cavala com molho de vilão) is an unusual but interesting combination. Limpets (lapas), served in their shells in a puddle of garlic butter are an anywhere, any time kind of dish that tastes not unlike snails. Cataplana is a delicious casserole of seafood combining prawns, squid, clams and white fish cooked with herbs and accompanied with rice.

In spite of this apparent abundance of seafood, the fact of the matter is that the oceanic waters surrounding Madeira are far too deep to support the shallow water species usually found in European restaurants. Much of those species – lobster, crab, mussels, oysters, clams,

Below: The many seafront cafés and brasseries in Funchal offer excellent dishes of the day in addition to a plentiful standard menu; eat in the open air at very reasonable prices.

Above: Island-grown garlic and chillies are key ingredients in traditional cooking on Madeira, and one or other crops up in most dishes, especially seafood.

even sea bass and sole, are all shipped from as far away as France or Ireland. That is not to say however that what you find in Madeiran restaurants will be any less fresh; like most of Europe, fish and seafood is generally farmed, frozen or shipped in alive. Here on Madeira, fresh fish is limited to the ubiquitous scabbard fish, parrot fish and not much else, although trout is farmed on the island. Local seafood is restricted to winkles and limpets, and, to be honest, you can live without those.

When looking for a good place to eat seafood there are a couple of pointers. First, there will be a visible abundance of perishable produce, a large aquarium, for example, full of live crabs and lobsters. This is an excellent sign; no restaurant owner in his right mind would invest in such stock without a regular and loyal customer base to consume it. Second, there are the customers themselves. A few restaurants have no need to rely on tourist trade because they serve high quality food that the Madeirans like. So, look for a restaurant full of locals and not many tourists, like O Barqueiro (*see* page 150).

The most frequently found meat dish is espetada, which comprises cubes of meat (usually beef), onions, tomatoes and peppers cooked over a wood fire. It is often served on skewers that hang from an iron frame at your table. Pork spiced with wine and garlic (Carne de vinho e alhos) is another popular dish, as is Cozido Madeirense, a tasty dish with boiled pork, chicken, steak, vegetables, sweet potato and rice.

Unlike meat, which has to be imported, fruit is plentiful and usually locally grown: pittanga, loquat and tomarillo are fruits most people will not know, but if the sense of adventure is lacking then passion fruit, kiwi, mango, banana, papaya, custard apples, guava and fig will more than compensate.

Bolo do Caco, a local speciality, is a round, flat bread, made with wheat flour and cooked on a tile (a caco to Madeiran people). You can often buy this from roadside 'bakeries', wood-fuelled griddles, where local women spend the morning preparing fresh bread – often served liberally spread with garlic butter, and delicious while

still hot. Pão de batata is a brown bread made with sweet potato. What might be thought of as 'normal' white bread is quite dense and heavy compared with other European white bread, and tastes a little doughy. Madeiran pastry, on the other hand, is a kaleidoscope of all things that should be forbidden, from the eponymous, dark and luscious Madeira, or honey cake (bolo de mel), sugar cane molasses biscuits, small cheesecakes and fennel candies.

Nor do the desserts relax the calorie-laden temptation of Madeira, although desserts are not normally eaten by Madeirans: even so, papaya pudding with caramel topping is irresistible, as is velvet pudding, a sweet made mainly with eggs. But in the main, desserts in restaurants are often an afterthought and generally (although increasingly less so) limited to fruit or ice creams.

Many of the old recipes of Madeira have been preserved and tweaked by today's chefs, passed from generation to generation like some priceless heirloom. If it's the traditional food of Madeira produced in the traditional way that you seek, then you need to explore the small villages, and be prepared to sample anything. Depending on the season you can still get boganga, a kind of pumpkin soup, the ubiquitous tomato and onion soup (which is actually rather more filling than you might imagine, and often contains a poached egg) and atum com milho frito (tuna with fried corn). Some of the better restaurants also serve açorda in a variety of guises – seafood is wonderful – which generally combines rice, fish and coriander.

Any dishes that are 'á la Madeira' are prepared with Madeira wine, which infuses a distinctive character and fragrance; they are all elegant, delicious and well worth seeking out.

Remarkably, for an island that has limited resources in terms of home-grown produce; few cattle, no sheep, for

Left: Mouth-watering desserts. With a plentiful bounty of fresh fruit to work with the culinary artists of Madeira know exactly how to titillate your palate. The safest option is to decline the Dessert Menu – but you'll regret it!

Popular Drinks

Poncha: Ideal in cold weather, Poncha combines rum, honey and lemon juice.

Nikita: Popular around Câmara de Lobos, Nikita blends white wine, ice cream, pineapple and sugar in a centrifugal machine.

Quentinha: Coffee, rum, sugar and lemon peel is perfect at Christmas. Well, any time really.

Pé de Cabra: A mixture of dry white wine with black beer, sugar, lemon peel and chocolate powder.

Sangria: Best served chilled on a hot day, Sangria blends red wine, lemonade, orange juice, sugar and assorted fruit – orange, lemon, apple – and peppermint leaves.

Cortadinho: For people who can't decide between dry white wine or coffee, Cortadinho combines the two, and adds lemon peel for zest.

Cidra: Similar to English cider (but not quite), Cidra has low alcohol and is very refreshing on hot days.

Liqueurs: For something with more of a kick, the Madeirans are particularly adept at turning virtually anything, even the most common of fruits, into a semi-lethal liqueur: peppermint, cherries, chestnuts, passion fruit, almonds, walnuts, banana and even eucalyptus seeds. Drink the Madeiran liqueurs sitting down and when you don't have far to go!

example, and with many ingredients having to be imported, the talent of Madeiran chefs nevertheless shines through in their creativity and imagination, and the attention they lavish on their dishes. You may not find the huge variety of ingredients associated with mainland Europe, but the chefs of Madeira don't let that stop them.

Sweet Temptations

As a rule, Madeirans are not over-bothered with desserts, and most restaurants tend to pay lip service to the notion – although the sabayon at the Casa Portuguesa (*see* page 154) makes you wish you'd had it as a starter and main course as well as dessert.

But there is one treat that the Madeirans probably don't want you to know about: the Fábrica de Santo António on the Travessa do Forno in Funchal is a classic example of a destination that draws the locals and is a target for discerning visitors. For over 100 years, the factory's famous honey cake, its biscuits, cookies and fennel drops are a legend. The factory has remained in the same premises throughout its existence, nor has it ever changed hands. Today, it is the oldest of its kind, operating under a semi-artisan regime. Everything inside the factory, with the exception of the wood-burning ovens, is original, and the recipes, some of which originate in England, are the same today as when they were first introduced.

Visit the factory shop and you instantly see why this is such a popular place: it exudes charm laced with friendly service. They never advertise; they don't need to. Nor do they restrict themselves to tried and trusted recipes; new ideas are evolving all the time, not least a range of diet biscuits (if that isn't an oxymoron) and delicious jams made from the island's abundant fruit harvests. Try it for yourself, and see if you can come away empty handed.

Madeira Wine

When the American Declaration of Independence was signed in 1776, the ceremony was sealed with a glass of Madeira wine, and Madeira is still used to toast anyone prestigious enough to be appointed a Freeman of the City of London. George Washington is said to have consumed a pint of Madeira each night with his dinner. Remarkably, the wine owes its success to the primitive shipping conditions of the 17th century: to reach the New World, the wines passed through the tropics, and the baking it received from the sun, gave an otherwise light and acidic wine, a softness, depth of flavour, and a pleasant burnt quality. By the late 1700s, orders were given to put pipes (a 'pipe' being 418 litres) of Madeira in the hold of ships as ballast, and send them on round trip voyages to all parts of the world, something of a wacky way to mature wine. Such well-travelled wine became known as Vinho da roda or 'Wine of the round voyage'. Why these wines

were not ruined, exposed as they were to constant rocking and extreme heat, is a mystery.

In 1815, the ship carrying Napoleon to exile in St Helena called in Funchal, where the British consul gave the ex-emperor a pipe of 1792 vintage wine. On reaching St Helena, the house Napoleon was supposed to occupy was not yet ready, and so he lodged with a local English family, one that had quite a taste for the wine, consuming almost a bottle a day. Napoleon's wine, however, was considered too young, and remained unopened, and stayed that way until well after his death. Eventually, the Napoleon Madeira found its way back to Funchal, and was sold to Blandy's, who put it into demijohns in 1840. One of these authentic 1840 demijohns was opened for Winston Churchill in the 1950s, during his brief stay, a gesture that so moved the great man that he personally poured a glass for all the guests at the table, and made sure that they understood the significance of this particular wine, pointing out that the wine was produced when Marie-Antoinette was still alive.

Two things conspired to help the growth of Madeira wine. As Portugal's possessions expanded westwards to the Americas, it was found that Brazil was able to produce better and cheaper sugar, until then a mainstay of the Madeiran economy. So, in the late 1500s the Madeiran farmers decided that wine was a more profitable crop.

Secondly, situated in the Atlantic shipping lanes, Madeira was a perfect staging post for ships travelling to the Americas or south around Africa. As a result, most

Right: The reputation of Madeiran wine spreads across the world and was used to toast the sealing of the American Declaration of Independence in 1776. Napoleon had a taste for it, too, as did Churchill. Sercial and Verdelho are dry wines, ideal as an aperitif, while Boal and Malvasia work best as end-of-meal drinks. Madeira has been a stopping-off point since the 16th century when sailors would take barrels of the precious wine on board. Madeira wine is quite used to travelling around the world; this was the natural way of making it taste even better.

ships dropped anchor in Funchal Bay, and invariably loaded wine for the voyage. What cinched the deal was a 17th-century British law forbidding the export of European wines to British colonies other than through British ports and in British ships. The one exception was Madeira, which became a regular supplier of wine to all American ships heading home.

America developed a huge appetite for the wine and became one of Madeira's most important customers, buying nearly a quarter of all the wine produced. By the 18th century, it was the only wine the British American and West Indian colonies would drink. News of its popularity in America created connoisseurs of Madeira in Britain, too, to the point that ladies were known to use it to perfume their handkerchiefs.

Today, the production of wine is hugely important to the island's economy, and one of the key features for which Madeira has long been renowned. Prince Henry 'the Navigator' is believed to have initiated the introduction of the first vines to Madeira during the early period of colonization. Later, wine production was carried out by Jesuit priests, who owned large areas of land, and imposed social and spiritual influence on the islanders. But the greatest aid to the infant wine industry was initiated by the British during the 18th century, from when wine was exported in quantities up to 20,000 barrels per year. These days, the island produces over five million bottles of Madeira wine annually.

The main areas for wine production are Câmara de Lobos, São Vicente and Santana where the grape varieties sercial, verdelho, boal, malvasia and tinta negra mole are planted. Almost 30% of the vineyards are dedicated to the production of red and white wine, which since 1999 has held the denomination VQPRD Madeirense. The first wines with this prized appellation came onto the market in 2000.

Today there are many varieties of the classic fortified Madeiran wine, so versatile in fact that they can be

__Below:__ The Madeira Wine Festival is celebrated at the time of the year when grapes are being harvested, in September. In Câmara de Lobos, the festival begins with the actual picking of the grapes. For tourists and locals alike the wine making ritual –carrying the grapes to the press, pressing of the grapes and all the traditions of a typical Madeira feast – is an excuse to party and celebrate. In the centre of Funchal, the Wine Festival includes light, sound and folk shows, all related to old wine-making traditions.

served at any time of day and with virtually any food. In many ways it is not unlike the French Pineau des Charentes, a blend of wine and brandy, but the process of making Madeiran wine, which involves heating the casks to aid preservation (known as estufalgem), also introduces a slightly burnt, somewhat caramelized, flavour which makes it a little stronger than pineau.

The dry wines – sercial and verdelho – are delicious as a chilled aperitif, while the sweeter wines – boal and malvasia – best accompany desserts. Sercial is a grape introduced from Portugal, and produces the lightest and softest Madeiran. It is planted mainly around Seixal, Ribeira da Janela, Jardim da Serra, Ponta da Pargo and Arco de São Jorge.

Verdelho was grown in Portugal before the 15th century, and is today planted around Funchal, Câmara de Lobos, Estreito da Câmara de Lobos and São Vicente. Originally from Bordeaux in France, boal produces a medium-sweet, full-bodied wine, and is grown around

Above: For the wine connoisseur, there are rare treats to be found as bottles of vintage Madeira (dating as far back as 1772) come onto the market. It won't be cheap, but it will be excellent. The Madeira Wine Museum is an excellent place to learn about the different wines.

Making Madeira Wine

After harvesting, the grape crop is taken to Funchal for fermentation, a stage that lasts for up to six weeks. Next, the wine is matured in 'warming rooms', heated to a temperature of around 45°C (113°F); this is the process known as estufalgem, following which the wine is left to rest for three months. The vintage wines (vinhos de canteiro) are warmed naturally, by the sun. Each lot is then left to rest for two years in oak barrels before blending, when brandy is added to fortify the wine until it reaches an alcohol level of 18–20%.

Câmara de Lobos, Ponta do Pargo and Calheta. The first vines planted in Madeira were malvasia, which produce a sweet wine with a good bouquet, but they are not favoured by modern wine producers. The workhorse of wine production, accounting for 60% of all wine production, is tinta negra mole which was developed from a cross between pinot noir and Grenache varieties. It is found around Câmara de Lobos, Funchal and São Vicente.

The richest of all the Madeiran wines, Malmsey, is a perfect after-dinner drink, although consumption should not be taken to the lengths adopted by the Duke of Clarence, who, under sentence of death in the Tower of London, chose to be drowned in a barrel of Malmsey.

Of the non-fortified wines, Madeira, traditionally producing just Seiçal and Enxurros, both of which carry the VQPRD appellation, is now pouring its energy into producing a wider range quality white wines to the extent that it is possible for restaurants to offer a good selection of wines solely produced on Madeiran soil; though many have yet to do so.

The Madeira Wine Company was a pioneer in this field when it produced its pale citrus, medium bodied, aromatic and very palatable Atlantis Branco in 1994, made with verdelho grapes. Sadly, that wine is no longer available, but others, also using the verdelho grapes, have come to fill the space its demise created, notably Casa da Vinha, which exudes fine aromas of lemon and passion fruit, and was the overall winner in the second Madeira White Wine Show. A year earlier it was Seiçal, a light blend of verdelho and arnsburger grapes, which stole the show. That German arnsburger grape, well adapted to the Madeiran climate and ripening early, also produces Rocha Branca, a very more-ish medium-bodied white.

Quinta do Moledo and Quinta do Moledo Reserva are really impressive wines produced on the northeast of the island around Arco de São Jorge in the crater of an extinct

Below: *With so many wines to choose from it's a good idea to spend some time relaxing in the bars, which have a convivial atmosphere offering the chance to socialize with local people and get to know more about the island's culture.*

volcano. The full-bodied quality of these wines comes from partial fermenting in new French oak barrels.

Experimentation goes on: the 2004 harvest brought the only white wine produced from the malvasia grape, the Reis da Cunha. The following year, the wine maker added some arnsburger grapes to the production to refresh the sweetness of the malvasia grape. Away from the tourists, the north of the island, around Ponta Delgada and Boaventura, there are extensive vineyards of verdelho and arnsburger which together produce a white Enxurros. And entering the market in 2006 is a new Madeiran wine, Vinha da Palmeira, produced around Câmara de Lobos, and using a blend of boal, verdelho and arnsburger grapes. All of which goes to show that the Madeiran wine makers are not resting on their laurels; Madeiran wines are increasing each year, and starting to rival many of those imported from mainland Portugal.

The wine harvest begins in mid-August, usually in Câmara de Lobos, and gradually works its way around the island before ending in Santana towards the end of September, an occasion that is celebrated with one huge island-wide party. There is a tradition that the first grapes were trodden by children. Whether that still happens is almost irrelevant; this is a time for celebration, and celebrate is what the Madeiran people do with gusto.

Dining Out

Restaurants are generally open every day from noon until 15:00, and in the evening from 18:00 until 23:00 (but in more rural locations often only until 21:00). It is usually not necessary to book, other than at the the top restaurants; just turn up, if there isn't a table free, wait at the bar or come back later. Madeiran and Portuguese people tend to eat later than northern Europeans, taking lunch between 13:00 and 15:00, and dinner between 20:00 and 21.30. Getting there ahead or after these times is always a good idea, although it may be difficult to get a meal after 22:00 in some of the rural towns and villages.

As well as fine international dishes, Madeira's restaurants are especially adept at providing hot and cold buffets embracing everything from pâté to shellfish. Funchal, in particular, has restaurants to suit all tastes; from modern, air-conditioned temples of dining with spectacular views, to more intimate, cosy taverns with rustic decoration and unfussy food. Do not overlook the superb restaurants that are a feature of many of the fine hotels; almost all are open to non-resident visitors, and offer a relaxing alternative to town centre eateries for a special occasion with the added bonus of being able to spend a few delightful hours in the embrace of botanical gardens, fine antiques and splendid settings.

Most restaurants serve what might be regarded as traditional Madeiran cuisine, the same dishes recurring, but with subtle variations, whichever restaurant you choose. In Funchal, you can eat amazingly well and inexpensively at any of the café/restaurants along the harbour front (Avenida do Mar), and should try at least one of them (see page 150). Take care not to allow yourself to be pressured by keen front-of-house touts trying to persuade you to dine with them; take your time and check out the menus and prices, especially if you are buying seafood, for example, lobster, which is priced by weight, and have to be imported.

At lunchtime in particular consider the 'Dish of the Day' (Menu do dia), on offer at many restaurants. These tend to be fairly simple and inexpensive dishes, mainly fish or pork, but accompanied by a fresh green salad are an ideal and light meal for the middle of the day.

Desserts, it has to be said, are not a strong point, and the choice in many restaurants is limited although there are a few that go beyond the fruit, ice cream and crème caramel basics, Casa Portuguesa (page 154) being a case in point.

Multilingual menus, usually in Portuguese, French, German and English, are the norm, and many waiters speak all these languages very well, and are happy to advise on dishes and wine.

Bars

Bars tend to open any time after 08:00, although at that end of the day it is mainly to serve coffee and pastries; the real drinking doesn't start until much later, and can continue into the early hours. Madeiran people generally restrict their drinking to the bars, and it is rare to see anyone drinking in the streets, although there is occasional evidence that the younger element find their own favourite places away from bars and restaurants.

Restaurants

With a fairly limited palette to work with, for many years the chefs of Madeira copped out and stuck to tried and trusted dishes that required little imagination. That is still the case in many parts of the island. But, championed by the head chefs in the best hotel restaurants, Madeira's culinary pedigree is getting better by the year. No longer is it just the luxury palaces of dining that offer the best; now quality restaurants are opening up everywhere, and proving hugely popular. And dining out no longer needs to cost a fortune. But be wary of high-priced, imported food, like lobsters and other shellfish.

Right: Dine in splendour at the Quinta da Bela Vista.
Quality restaurants are increasing yearly in Madeira,
pioneered by the seriously talented chefs in hotel restaurants.
Residence at the hotels is not a prerequisite of dining,
but a willingness to appreciate the cuisine is.
Just be sure to book in advance.

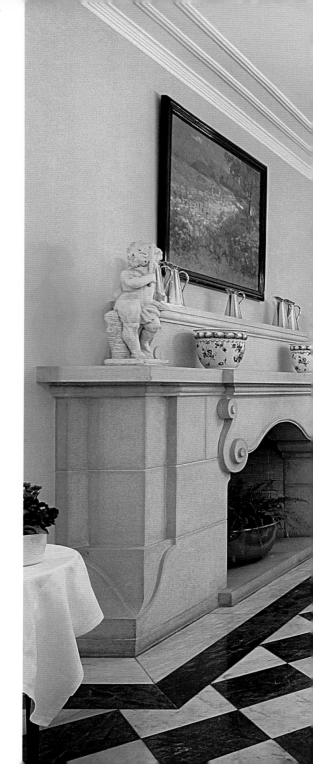

Funchal
Xôpana €€€€

Hopefully destined to become the first Madeiran restaurant to gain a coveted Michelin star, since opening in 2003, the restaurant at the exclusive Choupana Hills resort has acquired a reputation for its Asian-inspired cuisine. In recent times, that has changed somewhat and today there are three alternative menus: a gourmet option that focuses on contemporary dishes inspired by local cuisine; a healthy menu for diet conscious clients, and a reinvigorated Asian fusion menu. Arguably the finest restaurant on the island, and, as a result very popular. Reservations essential.

O Casa Velha €€€

One of the forerunners in the changing face of fine dining on Madeira, the dining room at the Casa Velha do Palheiro is part of the Blandy estate, so it should come as no surprise to find that all the Madeira wines in the house are from Blandy's. This is a semi-formal dining experience serving both à la carte and 'Tasting' menus, mainly Mediterranean. The quality of the food is excellent, but the choice of wine is very limited, and the wine list does not do the restaurant justice.

O Barqueiro €€€

The most varied fish restaurant on the island, and very popular with locals – which is always a good sign. Although you can get meat dishes here, this is the place to come for fish. The ambience is informal and the service efficient. The variety of fresh fish on offer is much greater than can be caught in Madeiran waters, but you will get superbly prepared parrot fish (bodião),

golden bream (pargo) and meaty grouper (garoupa). If you can't resist the experience of winkles (caramujos) or limpets (lapas), then this is the place to have them in style. You can often have a 'tasting' menu, in case you can't make your mind up.

Casa Mãe, Quinta Bela Vista (*see* page 109) €€€–€€€€

Serving a fusion of modern European and Madeiran cuisine, with daily à la carte menus, the quality of the Casa Mãe cannot be faulted, nor the talent of its experienced Madeiran chef who produces such delights as lobster and avocado salad with mango sauce, grilled bodião (parrot fish) with yoghurt, pickled pork and smoked ham risotto, passion fruit soufflé, and daily vegetarian dishes. Set this is a plush dining room amid fine art and antiques, add an extensive cellar of fine Portuguese and Madeiran wines, and top it off with knowledgeable and friendly service, and the Bela Vista offers a dining experience that is relaxed and informal, sumptuous and quite simply delightful.

Seafront Restaurants
Mar Azul €–€€

The waiters touting for your custom outside the Mar Azul tempt you into thinking that maybe business isn't so good, but the food here is excellent and good value, so long as you avoid the imported items.

Marina Terrace €–€€

On the northern edge of the marina, this restaurant serves everything from prize lobster to quiche lorraine and pizza. It can get quite musical as the staff are often in Madeiran costume, with live folk dancing and the plaintive fado music through the week.

Beer House €–€€

Well worth visiting if only for the excellence of its beer brewed on the premises, served by the glass or on tap with a one-metre pipe placed at your table; you can also take it away in five-litre kegs. They even have Giraffe beer, which presumably has a long neck! The food is pretty good, too, specializing in seafood specialities like Açorda de gambas (prawn and bread stew); just a little basic, but well prepared. Located at the eastern end of the harbour, and looking a little like a tented village, the Beerhouse also serves traditional non-fishy Madeiran cuisine.

Below: *The Casa Portuguesa Restaurant is typical of a growing trend in small restaurants serving high quality food. Set in the Old Town, this modest frontage belies the quality of the dining experience inside. Polite, friendly and knowledgeable service makes the experience all the more agreeable. Beware the sabayon!*

Fu Hao €

Tucked into the back of the Marina Shopping Centre, this excellent Cantonese-cum-Chinese-cum-Hong Kong eatery is ideal when the need for strong spices, that seldom feature in traditional Madeiran cuisine, becomes a craving. It's not that the food is especially strongly flavoured, but sometimes you get a hunger for something with a bit of a kick. You can get it here, very well prepared, and at ridiculously cheap prices. The quality of the cooking is consistently good, and it is worth dropping in here for lunch or an early evening meal. The restaurant offers a wide range of dishes, but this is much as you might expect. Avoid seafood, as this can be expensive.

Funchal Old Town

There are many restaurants in the Old Town, most are 'much of a muchness', but a few sing out, and the number of quality restaurants here is growing each year.

Casa Portuguesa €€–€€€

An absolute gem, tucked away in a side street in the Old Town; this is well worth searching for even though you'll have to run the gauntlet of the restaurant touts to get there. Imaginative and perfectly prepared Madeiran cuisine of the highest order, including an irresistible sabayon – if you get as far as desserts. Unlike many so-called 'gourmet' restaurants, the chef in Casa Portuguesa ably demonstrates how well the comparatively limited range of ingredients available to the island can be successfully prepared.

Gavião Novo €€–€€€

The reputation of the Rua de Santa Maria with its seedy bars may deter you from visiting No. 131; but it should not. This small restaurant specializes in Madeiran, mainly fish, cuisine of the freshest kind, although they do have some expensive imported items. Don't be surprised or affronted to be accosted by someone wielding a plate of fish; they're simply inviting you in for lunch or dinner. Often preceded by a complimentary glass of Madeiran wine, and followed, perhaps, by a glass of passion fruit liqueur, lunch at the Gavião Novo, is a pathetic, but perfectly understandable, excuse for doing very little in the afternoon; the food really is good, whatever you choose. Unlike most Funchal restaurants, this is a family-owned business; if they offer badly cooked food, the whole family is out of work.

Previous page: The restaurant at Quinta Splendida is deliciously extravagant and luxurious with a delightful old world charm. The menu is excellent and wide ranging, and the dishes prepared to perfection. Attention to detail is crucially important here, so be prepared to be pampered and to dine at the pinnacle of Madeiran culinary achievement.

Estreito da Câmara de Lobos
Bacchus Restaurant, Hotel Quinta Estreito (*see* page 111) €€€

Set in the original mansion house, the Bacchus Restaurant offers a daily menu based on available ingredients, and serves contemporary European cuisine with dishes such as fish and mint terrine, oven-baked sea bream, chicken fillet with smoked ham, and chocolate and mint parfait.

Adega da Quinta €€

Part of the Quinta Estreito complex that includes the Bacchus Restaurant (*see* above), the Adega da Quinta is one of the finest lunch and dinner restaurants, serving traditional Madeiran cuisine like char-grilled salt cod, braised chicken in a pot, or the celebrated espetada, or 'kebab' skewer (in this case a very large skewer that hangs from an iron frame at your table) laden with beef or pork. Excellent selection of wines, and a splendid view over the vineyards to the Atlantic.

Casa da Vinha €€

Not far from the Adega da Quinta at Estreito da Câmara de Lobos is the Casa da Vinha. This small restaurant, specializing in fine Madeiran food, sits in the middle of a sloping vineyard from which it makes what can truthfully be called its own 'House Wine'. Casa da Vinha wine, a dry white produced from verdelho grapes, is very refreshing on a warm day, and an agreeable accompaniment to many dishes, although the restaurant has a good selection of other, mainly Portuguese wines. There is a small car park just before the entrance, which is along a vine-covered, unevenly cobbled driveway – you could try driving up to the restaurant, but this is not recommended.

Encumeada
Restaurant Eucalipto €€

Located just a few minutes to the south of the Boca da Encumeada, this excellent roadside halt – perfect for lunch – serves food you may well not find in many other places on the island – rabbit, for example, or local beef and pork dishes, as well as vegetable casseroles.

Caliço
La Perla, Hotel Quinta Splendida
(*see* page 117) €€€

Quinta Splendida has a long-standing tradition of serving innovative and gastronomic dishes using organically grown vegetables and herbs from the hotel's own kitchen garden. The restaurant is in the original 18th-century manor house at the heart of this huge hotel complex and is decorated with Madeiran antiquities and paintings. La Perla is renowned for its classic epicurean cuisine, and has received several awards from the Portuguese Gastronomic Society.

Santana
Restaurant O Colmo €€

Part of the hotel of the same name (*see* page 116), the O Colmo restaurant is a real find; a place to enjoy lunch with the locals. Serving traditional Madeiran cuisine, this family-run restaurant uses much of its own locally grown produce, and does so admirably well. It is worth coming to this corner of Santana for lunch just to sample the lamb stew, or the cod cooked in chef's own style. And they have a good wine list, and do a fine range of Madeiran fruit liqueurs.

Porto Santo
O Calhetas €€

Found in Calheta, at the end of the road that runs down to the southern tip of the island, this well-known fish restaurant has all the traditional fish dishes plus a few specialities of fish and rice stews. Diners staying overnight on the island will get some spectacular sunsets from here during the summer months.

Below: Lobster, crab and king prawn are available at many restaurants in Funchal and are perfect for a special celebration washed down with a fine Madeiran or Portuguese wine.

Surf and Turf

Left: *The natural swimming pools at Porto Moniz are a great attraction, offering bracing sea air and the saltiness of the sea without the perils of crashing waves.*

One of the main reasons for visiting Madeira – apart from the year-round mild climate, the fresh sea air, the natural history, the folklore, the history and legends, the excellent food and wine and a long tradition of welcoming visitors from Europe – is for the walking. This is outstanding walking country, a place of massive landscapes and daunting ravines across which ingenuity has composed amazing routes. Madeira deserves the attention of serious walkers everywhere.

But this is a splendid place too for a range of sports – golf, cycling, adventure sports, diving, paragliding ...

Left: The heart of Madeira is the province of walkers, and trails network the rugged landscape offering breathtaking views of the whole island.

Walking

There can't be many places in Europe where you can take a bus ride to around 1500m (4922ft), way up in the mountains, jump out for a snack, and then take off to two higher peaks along a fabulous mountain ridge walk. But on Madeira you can.

Not only does Madeira offer the walker a fantastic selection of walking routes, it also has a superb range of environments from rugged volcanic coastal walking to high mountains with subtropical forest, highland moorland and steep gorges. And across all these different terrains run the levadas.

Levadas are watercourses with adjacent footpaths, which penetrate virtually every part of the mountainous heartland of Madeira. Built originally in the 15th century using slave or convict labour working with little more than pickaxes, chisels and bare hands, the levadas take some frighteningly daredevil routes across mountainsides, often high above steep valley sides or rocky precipices, frequently passing through tunnels. Not only do they irrigate the many fields and terraces, but also supply water to the island's electricity generating power stations.

The levadas are maintained by the Madeiran government, which employs teams of levadeiros, who patrol the watercourses, clearing debris and rockfall, and repairing any storm damage. The levadeiro is also responsible for operating the sluices that channel water to the various farmsteads, which are charged for the service. It is the system of paths originally built for maintenance that have proven a valuable source of income for the island economy, as visitors have come to realize that walking the levadas is an exhilarating way of appreciating the Madeiran landscape and of viewing its high mountains without any of the effort normally associated with mountain climbing. As the gradient of the levadas is gentle, and mainly follows contours, it means that the accompanying path is much the same, making them easy to walk, although in quite a few places both the levada and the path become very narrow, surprisingly steep and often directly above steep drops.

The best time of year for walking is from July to the end of September; this is when rain is less likely and the skies generally clear, and in the mountains the temperatures tend to be rather cooler. In June you may find more clouds, especially around the coast, and rainy periods can make some of the paths very slippery. And whatever the time of year there is always the possibility of cloud forming in the afternoons, especially at altitude, so an early start is always advised.

For the most part, walking on the island is within the ability of any regular walker accustomed to British and European terrain, but it is essential to bring appropriate footwear and the usual walking clothing and equipment,

Left: Start of the main tail linking Pico Arieiro and the highest point of the island, Pico Ruivo (far right). This route is excellent but demanding.

Above: *The ingenuity of those who built the levadas is evident enough, but tunnels like this one, near Rabaçal at the western edge of the Paúl da Serra, raise the bar on construction skills.*

Reading Matter

A useful guide to the levadas and walking in Madeira generally (including Porto Santo), is 'Walking in Madeira' by Paddy Dillon (Published by Cicerone Press – www. cicerone.co.uk) which provides guidance to 50 mountain, coastal and levada walks.

among which you may find a torch a useful aid, as some of the levadas disappear into tunnels for a while.

If you are not wholly confident about walking on your own, consider taking a guided walk. Quite a few of the hotels organize walking trips, or can put you in touch with walking tour operators, who will collect you from your hotel, organize packed lunches (if you remember to ask), and drop you off at the end of a half day or full day's walking.

Golf

Madeira has two high quality golf courses, both set in stunning locations: Santo da Serra, a 27-hole course that hosts the Madeira Open Championship, and Palheiro Golf. Golfers with limited experience can take lessons at both courses. Here the golfing high season starts in October and permits constant playing throughout the winter.

The Santo da Serra is closely linked with the nearby Quinta Serra Golfe (*see* page 119), which offers special rate packages for visitors who are staying at the hotel and playing golf.

Santo da Serra Golf Club, ranked as one of the top 100 courses in Europe, is also one of the most spectacular, with staggering views from the mountains to the sea below. Designed by Robert Trent Jones, its 27 holes are all characterized by generous fairways, tight, undulating greens, and a choice of tee positions to suit all abilities. It is situated at 700m (2297ft) above sea level, and several holes have very distracting views over sheer drops down to tiny villages, or across the sea to the ghostly Desertas floating across the horizon. One of the most memorable holes is the fourth on the Machico loop, a modest 179m, but a hole that requires utmost concentration and a long carry over a deep chasm to a well-guarded green, where even a par is a good result; the sort of hole, in fact, that golfers love to hate.

Palheiro Golf is situated in the hills to the east of Funchal, boasting fantastic views over the bay and the city. This 18-hole, 6000-metre+ course was designed in 1993 by Cabell Robinson, and is skillfully set within the

parkland of the Quinta de Palheiro Ferreiro. Winding its way through former farmland and forest, and remarkable for tight fairways, fast greens, and judicious use of the exotic trees that once covered the entire hillside, the course is a worthy challenge for all handicap levels. Unusually, Palheiro has five par-3's and five par-5's, one of which, the final, 487-metre hole, is a gambler's downhill dogleg right, risk/reward challenge, where the brave might reach the green in two.

There is also a fine 19-hole course on Porto Santo, the design of the Spanish golf supreme Severiano Ballesteros. This course, opened in 2004, is more challenging than the courses on Madeira, and is designed in marked contrast to the barren landscape that surrounds it. This is not a course for novices, who are prohibited, but experienced golfers will find interest and no doubt frustration in the contorted and ingenious design. There are six par-3's, six par-4's (all long) and six par-5's; sea breezes are an added handicap here, especially on the back nine, and on holes 13 to 15, which are alongside the cliffs.

Diving
Madeira
There are a number of sites around Madeira where scuba diving is possible, and some hotels can arrange diving sessions, usually in the waters around Garajau and Caniço de Baixo or Machico.

To hire equipment you need to show a diving certificate and log book. Most places can arrange PADI diving courses for beginners. There are new dive clubs and schools setting up annually in Madeira.

Manta Diving Center is the only base in the underwater national park of Madeira, and only a few steps

Previous page: Santo da Serra's 27-hole golf course is by far the island's finest, but sometimes plagued by mountain mists.
Right: Paragliding is a developing activity on Madeira, but most hotels can book flights and training for visitors.
Below: The clear (and deep) waters that surround Madeira and Porto Santo are increasingly popular with divers: a chance to meet the fish face-to-face before they arrive on your plate.

The potential for diving around Porto Santo, and the value of dive tourism, prompted the authorities in 2000 to sink a huge cargo ship, the Madeirense. Lying on a sandy bottom at 34m (112ft) and around a mile out of Porto Santo, this is a deservedly popular dive site. The wreck is in good condition, and for those with the relevant experience it is possible to explore the interior, although the size of the wreck – 70m (230ft) – means that two dives are better for comfort.

Porto Santo also offers other dive sites ranging from offshore reefs with superb underwater scenery to caves and even an archaeological dive off the island of Cal.

Porto Santo Sub is a PADI resort and TDI facility with two boats and two compressors and 40, 12 litre/220 bar tanks. It is possible to rent all equipment. There are 20 dive sites available ranging from 8–60m (26–197ft). Courses are also available.

Paragliding

Adventure junkies are increasingly heading to Madeira to take advantage of the island's newest craze, paragliding. There is a long way to go yet before Madeira ranks alongside Alpine and Pyrenean destinations for paragliding, but those enthusiasts who do make the journey are finding that Madeira has much to offer.

Paragliding first began in Madeira in 1990, when the Aero Club da Madeira invited a Portuguese pilot to join them; this became the maiden paragliding flight in Madeiran air. Because Madeira is a small island, flights tend to be shorter and lower than on mainland Europe, and are technically less demanding. But throw into the balance the fabulous visibility and uncrowded skies, and it's easy to see why more paragliders are finding Madeira such an attraction.

Boat Trips and Sea Watching

Almost every day is the same: at 10:00 and 15:00, a small Armada of sailing boats set off to scour the coast for sighting of dolphins, whales, turtles and oceanic birds. It's called 'Sea watching', and its popularity is immense. Calm seas and a little luck are needed to get

away from a domestic reef with a large number of fishes which you can discover by yourself, with a partner, or a guide. The centre has up-to-date rental equipment, maintained and checked by skilled personnel. Beginners and advanced students are trained according to CMAS and PADI.

Tubarão Madeira Mergulho has the following for rent: 50, 10 and 12 litre tanks in steel and aluminium; 20 complete sets of equipment in various sizes for women and men, plus NITROX and rebreather equipment; five complete sets of equipment for children and teenagers with tanks of four and seven litres; Uwatec-Computer Aladin Sport and NITROX; Sherwood and Scubapro regulators; Dräger Rebreather equipment; underwater camera; underwater lamps; signal buoy and signal rocket.

Porto Santo

The island of Porto Santo is gaining quite a reputation for diving holidays with dives to suit all levels of experience. The water is usually warm and visibility anything up to 30m (98ft), making this a fine all-year location.

the best from a trip, but when the skipper spots something and heads towards it, excitement mounts. Most often it will be dolphin that are especially abundant in the warm, food-rich waters around Madeira, but whale sightings are increasingly common, as are turtles, which sleep on the surface and are easily spotted. Four species of whale are regular visitors to Madeira: fin whale, sperm whale, Bryde's whale and sei whale; five species of turtle are here, too. Most sightings are of loggerhead turtles, but there have been several sightings of leatherback turtles, the largest of all the sea turtles.

Birds are also around in good numbers throughout the year, and sailing trips can include sightings of Cory's shearwater, Bulwer's petrels, Madeira petrels, band-rumped storm petrels and Fea's petrels, birds that arrive at the beginning of spring to nest on the archipelago, and tend to stay until autumn.

Deep-sea Fishing

When the Madeirans speak of 'Deep Sea', they mean really deep, and the offshore waters offer some of the world's best big game fishing, especially for Atlantic blue and white marlin (in season, June–September), which can weigh in at over 454kg (1000lb). June to September is also good for blue-eye tuna, while April to October see blue shark, hammerhead shark, barra-

Below: Dolphin, turtle and whale watching is a popular pastime, and numerous boat trips are available from Funchal, offering excursions of varying lengths, and almost always finding something to marvel at.

cuda, bonito and wahoo, with Manta rays appearing between August and October. Blue fin tuna appear in October and November.

Madeira is a signatory to the tag-and-release policy that sees fish being returned to the sea once photographed. Most of the fishing trips set off from Funchal.

Rallying Round
Madeira Wine Rally

In spite of its fascinating name, which conjures up images of endless days of obligatory wine tastings, the Madeira Wine Rally, now approaching its 50th year, is a high-speed, frantic, motorized dash around various parts of the island. For most people it is purely a spectator sport, with numerous vantage points from which to take in the action. The rally is always held in early August, and this is something to bear in mind if planning on travelling around the island at this time.

This rally is one of the most important trials of the European Championship, and also the most important

sporting event in the region, bringing world-famous rally drivers to Madeira, as thousands of people fill the mountain slopes in order to find a good viewing spot. Car rally aficionados rate this as one of the best tarmac competitions anywhere in the world.

Classic Rally

Less frenetic, Madeira's classic automobile club (CACM) hosts a rally of vintage cars each year at the end of June as part of the international vintage rallying scene, which means that the rally is restricted to original and perfectly conserved classic cars. Over the course of this four-day rally, the competitors cover more than 400km (249 miles) of Madeira's tortuous roads in an atmosphere that is rather more convivial than competitive.

On the Crest of a Wave: Surfing

The fantastic coastline of Madeira is an attraction to anyone, yet it shields one of the island's greatest secrets – this is also a superb surfing resort.

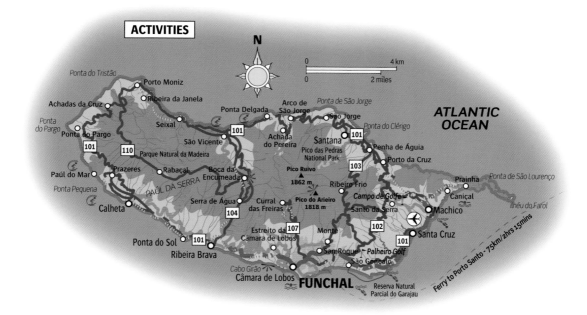

Curiously, given the growing popularity of surfing as a sport, the attractions of Madeira remained concealed from most of the world until the mid-90s, partly because of the difficulties in traversing the island to the various surfing spots, but also because no-one among the surfing fraternity had publicized what was possible here. True, accessibility to the surfing arenas depended then, as it does now, on the benevolence of Mother Nature, and catching the ultimate wave does call for a modicum of patience.

But the island's seas generate waves just as powerful and exciting as any in the rest of the world, and today the tiny village of Jardim do Mar has become intimately affected by the attentions of the surfing devotees. Along this delightful stretch of coastline, four- or five-metre waves roll in to the villages of Paul do Mar, the Ponta Pequena, and the more famous Ponta do Jardim.

Other parts of the island, too, offer excellent surfing potential, especially along the north coast where villages like Contreira, Ponta Delgada and São Vicente often provide surfers with good waves, albeit difficult to access.

The best surfing conditions occur in the summer months, when the sea's rhythm slows down, and the warm sun and higher water temperature combine to offer better conditions.

Beaches

If you are looking for palm-fringed golden sandy beaches, then Madeira has limited choice; the only golden beach, at Calheta, is imported. Madeira is a volcanic island, and its beaches are made up of dark volcanic sand, which nevertheless seems to enthrall young children. Even so, the island's beaches are

Right: Because of the island's volcanic origins, the sandy beach at Calheta is the only golden sand beach worthy of mention on Madeira, but it is immensely popular. Two beaches oppose one another across a small man-made inlet on the seafront.

popular for their high standards of cleanliness, crystal clear water and agreeable temperatures. However, the majority of Madeira's beaches are pebbled and can be rather uncomfortable.

Because of a different geological pedigree, nearby Porto Santo more than amply compensates for what could be seen as Madeira's shortfall. Here a great swathe of luxurious golden sand runs almost the entire length of the island, and visitors and locals alike flock here for day or weekend breaks.

Many people consider the sands of Porto Santo to be therapeutic, so don't be surprised to see people buried to the necks in the sand; it looks like a childish prank, but isn't.

Football

There are two top football teams based on Madeira: Maritimo, which plays in the top Portuguese league, and Nacional. Maritimo plays at the Barreiros Stadium, while Nacional plays in the Estádio E Rui Alves. Tickets for most matches can be bought from the stadiums, or from the club shops in Funchal.

Casino

The five-star Pestana Carlton Park Hotel is part of the complex that includes Madeira's highly popular and unique Casino, know to the locals as the 'Rack of Lamb'. The complex was designed by the Brazilian architect, Oscar Niemeyer, and is an understated masterpiece of modern design and fabrication, providing a sense of space and integration of natural light that are the outstanding characteristics of what is, in effect, a contemporary example of modern art. It is the only casino on the island.

Designed in lively colours and to the very highest standards, the casino offers an area dedicated to slot machines with more than 200 of the latest models. In addition, there are traditional gaming rooms

Left: The entrance to Madeira's only casino, at the Pestana Carlton Park Hotel.

with French and American roulette, Black Jack and chemin-de-fer.

The Palm Bar and the Rio Restaurant produce South American specialities until the early hours. There is also the Bahia Panoramic Restaurant where you can enjoy an international show while having your meal.

In the basement, the popular Copacabana Bar is decorated throughout in a tropical style and has a large dance floor. Here, a resident band provides live music, making this the ideal spot in Funchal to enjoy a good night's dancing.

Entertainment

The casino and the hotel offer their guests splendid entertainment for much of the week. On Wednesdays and Saturdays after a relaxed dinner, the resident band kicks off your evening with some memory-provoking renditions of all-time favourite songs, while exotic dancers take you on a journey through the music of the 50s to the 90s.

Thursday is Broadway Night, when dinner is followed by a spectacular show with songs and dances from Broadway and West End musicals.

The Friday evening cabaret show pulsates with heady rhythms and colour and glamour, closing with an explosive Can-Can performance.

Madeira for Families

The idea that Madeira is a destination for 'senior' citizens is a long-gone myth. Today, this vibrant and exciting island is a delight for people of all ages.

All the best hotels offer extra facilities for children, including games rooms, satellite TV, tennis, mini-golf, and it very soon becomes obvious that Madeiran people love children and give them friendly and sincere attention. There is nothing sinister in this; it is all perfectly genuine.

Madeira is a virtually crime-free destination, and, subject to modest safeguards, it is generally safe to let older children explore for themselves.

Travel Directory

Left: *All the mountain trails on Madeira are well signed, but a map and compass will still prove useful.*

So much is changing in Madeira and Porto Santo — new roads appear, as well as new apartment blocks, hotels and restaurants — that any specific information can become out-of-date remarkably quickly. In the event that any of the following information appears inaccurate, then up-to-date details can be obtained from the tourist office in Funchal.

Left: Post boxes outside the main post office in Funchal.

Practical Guide
Tourist Information
Tourist Offices
UK
Portuguese National Tourist Office
22-25a Sackville Street, London W1S 3EJ
tel: 020 7494 5720; fax: 020 7494 1868

Madeira
Funchal: Avenida Arriaga, 16, 9004-519 Funchal
tel: (+351) 291 211 902; fax: (+351) 291 225 658
info@madeiratourism.com
Open Mon–Fri 09:00–20:00, Sat–Sun 09:00–18:00.
Airport Tourist Office: Santa Catarina de Baixo,
9100 Santa Cruz
tel: (+351) 524 933.
Câmara de Lobos: Casa da Cultura de Câmara de Lobos,
Rua Padre Eduardo Clemente Nunes Pereira,
9300-116 Câmara de Lobos
tel: (+351) 291 943 470.
Caniço: 9125 Caniço de Baixo
tel: (+351) 291 932 919.
Machico: 9200 Machico
tel: (+351) 291 962 289.
Ponta do Sol: Centro de Observação de Natureza,
Lagoa – Lugar de Baixo, 9360-119 Ponto do Sol
tel: (+351) 291 972 850.
Porto Moniz: 9270 Porto Moniz
tel: (+351) 291 850 193.
Riberia Brava: Forte de São Bento, 9350 Riberia Brava
tel: (+351) 291 951 675.
Santana: Sitio do Serrado, 9230 Santana
tel: (+351) 291 572 992.

Porto Santo
Avenida Henrique Vieira e Castro, 9400 Porto Santo
tel: (+351) 291 982 361.

Be alert to the fact that many of the travel agents in Funchal promote themselves as tourist information points, but with the intention of persuading you to book on one of their organized tours. There is nothing wrong with this, as most of the tours (either in a minibus or on a coach) are good value for money. But the tour will include time for browsing in shops or taking lunch rather than sightseeing. If there are two or three of you in a group it may work out cheaper to book a taxi for the day (see 'Taxis'). It is certainly more flexible, you'll see more, and often see places the tour buses are unable to reach. More to the point, you can dictate where you want to go.

When to Go
Semi-permanent sunshine and a mild sub-tropical climate with average temperatures between 17°C (62°F) early in the year to 23°C (75°F) in autumn makes Madeira an all-year-round destination. If there is a peak season it's around Christmas and New Year (when hotel prices can go up by as much as 30%), while May and June tend to be comparatively quiet if a little cloudy. Low season is between the end of October and early December, or from late January to March. These also tend to be the wettest months, but if it does rain it rarely sets in for long.

Weather-wise Porto Santo is generally fine throughout the year, and enjoys its own micro-climate. Rainfall is low, and sunshine a constant feature, although, being a small island, it can be breezy.

How to Get There
Madeira
TAP Air Portugal (www.tap-airportugal.co.uk) and GB Airways (www.gbairways.co.uk) are the main carriers from the UK.

Charter flights with the tour companies are cheaper, but may not be available at peak times. It is always a good idea to book well ahead if planning to take 'Flight only' tickets with charter companies.

Flight costs can be evaluated and tickets booked through Madeira Portugal Ltd., 122 Tuckton Road, Tuckton, Bournemouth, Dorset BH6 3JX (tel: 01202 424466; info@madeiraportugal.co.uk; www.madeira-portugal.co.uk), or through local travel agents. Opodo is also a quick online way of finding the cheapest flights (www.opodo.co.uk).

Madeira's airport, Santa Catarina, was rebuilt in order to accommodate larger aircraft, and re-opened in 2000, with a new runway. The airport is 18km (11+ miles) from Funchal, and an Aerobus – free for TAP passengers on presentation of flight tickets (but otherwise a few euros per person) – runs to the city at roughly one- to two-hour intervals.

Madeira Airport, ANAM (Aeroportos e Navegação Aérea da Madeira), 9100-105 Santa Cruz; tel: (+351) 291 520 700; fax: (+351) 291 520 761; anam@anam.pt; www. anam.pt. There is free WiFi Internet connection in certain parts of the airport, along with currency exchanges, ATMs, information desk, tourist office, reservation office for rural tourism, left luggage, post office, travel agency, tour operator and VIP lounges.

Porto Santo

By air: There are regular 15-minute flights at one- or two-hour intervals from Madeira to Porto Santo. Check-in is not later than 45 minutes before departure, and tickets can be booked through travel agents or at the TAP Air Portugal office, Avenida do Mar, Funchal, tel: (+351) 291 239 211.

Although there are no buses from Porto Santo airport to the main town, Cidade Vila Baleira, there are plenty of taxis for the 10-minute journey.

ANAM (Aeroportos e Navegação Aérea da Madeira), Ilha do Porto Santo; tel: (+351) 291 980 120; Fax: (+351) 291 980 121; anam@anam.pt; www.anam.pt

By sea: A luxury ferry, equipped with cinema, restaurants, shops and games facilities, leaves Madeira daily. Departure times vary throughout the year, but generally the ferry leaves Madeira at 08:00, and Porto Santo at 19:00; these times change at weekends. On board it is worth upgrading to First Class, which offers a better view of where you're going, as well as cooked breakfast or evening meal, tea, coffee and fruit drinks.

Connecting buses from the ferry terminal on Porto Santo take five minutes to reach Cidade Vila Baleira, and there are often a number of taxis, too.

A day sailing to Porto Santo is very popular, with plenty of time to make the most of its golden beaches. Journey time is around 2 hours 30–45 minutes.

Tickets can be bought in advance from travel agents,

on the marine terrace or from the jetty just before sailing. For further information contact Porto Santo Line, Rua da Praia 4, Funchal, tel: (+351) 291 210 300. At busy periods, do not leave buying you ticket until the last moment; there won't be any.

Passports and Visas

If you are visiting Madeira from a European Union country belonging to the Schengen Agreement, there are no restrictions on entry. Visitors from countries that are not party to the agreement need identification, which, under Portuguese law, means a valid passport and, in some cases, a visa.

The name 'Schengen' originates from a small town in Luxembourg. In June 1985, seven European Union countries signed a treaty to end internal border checkpoints and controls. More countries have joined the treaty over the past years. At present, there are 15 Schengen countries, all in Europe: Austria, Belgium, Denmark, Finland, France, Germany, Iceland, Italy, Greece, Luxembourg, Netherlands, Norway, Portugal, Spain and Sweden. All these countries, except Norway and Iceland, are European Union members.

If you are unsure about any matter concerning your travel documents, please contact either your travel agent or the Portuguese Embassy/Consulate based in your home town.

Flights: Forbidden Items

For security reasons, the following items may not be carried in luggage:

- Explosives, arms, ammunitions, firecrackers
- Compressed gases
- Liquid and solid flammable substances
- Poisonous and infectious substances
- Corrosive and oxidizing materials
- Radioactive materials
- Magnetized materials
- Alarm devices
- Scissors, cutters and nail clippers (not allowed in hand luggage)

Embassies and Consulates

There are no embassies on Madeira, but there are the following consulates in Funchal.

Austria: Rua Imperatriz D. Amélia, Edificio Princessa Ljs 0/4, 9000-018 Funchal tel: (+351) 291 206 100.

Belgium: Praça do Municipio, 8-1° D, 9000-072 Funchal tel: (+351) 291 221 833.

Denmark: Rua do Paiol, No. 4, 9000-642 Funchal tel: (+351) 291 743 765.

Finland: Rua 31 de Janeiro, 15, 9050-011 Funchal tel: (+351) 291 234 871.

France: Avenida do Infante, 58, 9004-526 Funchal tel: (+351) 291 200 750.

Germany: Largo do Phelps, 6-1°, 9050-025 Funchal tel: (+351) 291 220 338.

Italy: Rua do Bom Jesus, 14, 9050-028 Funchal tel: (+351) 291 223 890.

Netherlands: Complexo Vila Porto Mare, Rua d Leichlingen, 5, 9000-003 Funchal tel: (+351) 291 703 803.

Norway: Rua das Maravilhas, 23, 9000-177 Funchal tel: (+351) 291 741 515.

Spain: Edificio América, Caminho do Amparo, Piornais S. Martinho, 9000-248 Funchal tel: (+351) 291 701 144.

Sweden: Rua Padre Gonçalves Câmara 26, 9000-085 Funchal tel: (+351) 291 233 603.

UK: Avenida Andar, 10, 9000-069 Funchal tel: (+351) 291 212 860.

USA: Rua da Alfandega, No. 10, 9000-059 Funchal tel: (+351) 291 235 636.

Customs

As a member of the European Union, Portugal (Madeira), is subject to customs regulations. There are limits on goods obtained duty free within the EU, and on goods bought outside the EU. Items bought within the EU for personal use are subject to guidelines which define quantities regarded as for personal use.

Drugs (other than medicinal), firearms and other weapons, obscene material and unlicensed animals are all prohibited.

Time Zone

Madeira operates to Greenwich Mean Time (GMT) in the summer, and, as in the rest of the EU, puts the clock back one hour at the end of October, and forward at the end of March.

Health Requirements

No special immunizations are required for visitors to Madeira. Emergency treatment at state hospitals is free of charge for European Union citizens, and there are good private health care services for visitors from other countries, and for non-emergency matters for EU citizens. So, it is vital to have private medical and travel insurance to cover the cost of emergencies. If you intend to claim against insurance, be sure to obtain and keep receipts.

Visitors from the UK should carry a European Health Insurance Card, which has replaced the former E111 forms. Information about the card is available from the UK National Health Service, tel: 0845 46 47 (UK only); www.nhsdirect.nhs.uk. Health-related travel advice is available by calling tel: +44 (0)20 7210 4850 (Mon–Fri, 09:00–17:00 UK time), or by visiting the website www. dh.gov.uk/travellers

Dentists

Dental services on Madeira are excellent, and dentists advertise in a number of free English and German magazines usually available in hotels, and the tourist information office in Funchal.

Pharmacists (Chemists)

Prescription and non-prescription drugs are available from pharmacies (farmâcia), but, if you need regular medication, it is better to take adequate supplies with you in case they are not available locally. Pharmacies open Monday to Friday (09:00–13:00 and 15:00–19:00), and Saturday (09:00–12:30); there is a late duty rosta posted in pharmacy windows.

It is worth remembering that the pharmacists in Madeira are allowed to prescribe suitable medicines for minor illnesses, and can thus save you the cost of a trip to a doctor.

Hospitals

The main hospital in Funchal for non-residents is Cruz de Carvalho, Avenida Luis Camões (tel: 291 705 600).

The main hospital on Porto Santo is the Centro de Saúde do Porto Santo (tel: 291 982 211).

Emergencies

For emergencies requiring fire, ambulance or police, telephone 112.

Personal Safety

There is a low crime rate on Madeira, but wherever wealth and poor standards of living are found close together, there is always temptation.

In the unlikely event that you are the victim of a crime in Funchal, report the incident to the main police station, on Rua Infância, 28 (tel: 291 208 400; in Porto Santo the main police station is at Sitio das Matas in Cidade Vila Baleira (tel: 291 982 423).

Remember to get a copy of a written statement to support any insurance claim you may wish to make on your return home.

There are some simple guidelines which may help minimize the impact of any crime:
• Avoid carrying too much cash
• If taking cash from an ATM, put your cash safely away before walking away from the machine, and, if possible, have someone standing with you
• Leave your valuables in your hotel – most have room safes, and these should be used
• Don't leave valuables in an unattended car, or on the beach
• Be aware that pickpockets may operate in crowded situations, like markets or on busy streets

The Basics
Business Hours

Shops: Mon–Fri 09:00–13:00 and 15:00–19:00; Sat 09:00–13:00. Many of the larger stores and retail outlets in the main tourist areas may stay open through the lunch period, and until 22:00. Most shops are closed on Sundays.

Shopping Centres: daily (including Sun) 10:00–22:00.

Pharmacies: usual opening hours, plus a 24-hour rosta, which is displayed on the door.

Museums: times vary, but 10:00–12:30 and 14:30–18:00 are the norm. Many of the museums have a closing day (usually Mon).

Offices: Mon–Fri 09:00–17:00.

Banks: Mon–Fri 08:30–15:00; some open on Saturdays 09:00–12:30.

Post offices: Mon–Fri 08:30–20:00; Sat 09:00–12:30. Reduced hours at small, urban and rural branches.

Electricity

The power supply on Madeira is 220 volts AC. Sockets accept two-pronged round-pin plugs. Adaptors for most countries are available at most departure airports. A transformer may be necessary for equipment operating on 100–120 volts.

Internet Connections

There is a growing number of Internet cafés, especially in Funchal, although don't be surprised to see them cropping up increasingly in more rural locations.

More often these days, hotels are offering a free Internet connection – usually just a single laptop or desktop machine at a communal location. Elsewhere, Internet connections are available for a charge, and some hotels offer Ethernet (LAN connections, and supply the cables) for a nominal daily rate; this is cheaper than connecting through a guest room telephone when even the most clued-up techy will still have to make a national call to Lisbon in Portugal to connect.

There are a number of companies offering worldwide Internet connection facilities, which means that you only have to dial to a local number rather than call to your home country for a connection. Try the website www.net2roam.com, and, provided you have your pop3 details (you need to get them from your server), you can usually collect your emails via www.mail2web.com

Money

The currency on Madeira is the euro (symbol €) which was introduced on 1 January 2002, replacing the old Portuguese escudo. Exchange rates are, of course,

Above: 'Dumb waiter' at the entrance to the Casa Portuguesa in Funchal Old Town. Welcome is exactly how you feel in this lovely eatery.

cost items. Coins are available as 1 or 2 euros, and 50, 20, 10, 5, 2 and 1 cents. Be sure to have a ready supply of the 1 and 2 euro and 50 cents coins, if only to feed parking meters.

All major credit cards are widely accepted in shops, restaurants and hotels, but Madeira has a strong cash-based economy, so don't be surprised to hear that 'There is a problem accepting foreign credit cards', followed by a request for cash payment. Travellers from outside the EU should be advised to notify their credit card company in advance of the likelihood of the card being used abroad.

Banks and ATM machines are found across the island, and it is unlikely that you will find yourself in a place where you cannot get currency. But many of the ATMs limit the amount per transaction, often to 200 euros.

Tipping

Tipping is not generally expected, although many restaurant bills will include service charge, and in a bar you can always leave any small change as a tip. Attendants in public toilets in Funchal expect a tip (*see* below).

A 10% tip for taxi drivers or for good service in a restaurant will always be appreciated. A 1-cent tip has been known to make a point on the very rare occasion that restaurant service has not been what it might.

Post Offices

There are post offices (Correios) in all the main towns and many of the villages, and postage stamps are often available at newsagents. Post boxes are red or blue, with blue being for international mail. The main post offices in Funchal are equipped to handle telegrams, telexes, faxes and telephone calls as well as mail.

Telephones

There are telephone kiosks on all the main streets in Funchal, and increasingly elsewhere across the island. Most bars and cafés have pay phones, although some only take phonecards.

International calls are expensive, especially from hotels; most dual- and tri-band mobile phones (except

variable, almost on a daily basis, and are displayed in all banks, currency exchanges and hotels. Notes are available in denominations of 500, 200, 100, 50, 20, 10 and 5 euros, although many establishments are reluctant to accept the higher denominations, especially for low

those from the USA) will work perfectly well on Madeira, with good coverage almost everywhere.

To call Madeira or Porto Santo from abroad dial 00 351 (the international dialling code for Portugal), then 291, the area code for both islands. In Madeira or Porto Santo you only need to dial the subscriber number, so you drop 00 351 and 291 from any of the numbers given in this chapter. International dialling codes are:

Australia	00 61
France	00 33
Germany	00 49
Irish Republic	00 353
New Zealand	00 64
South Africa	00 27
Spain	00 34
UK	00 44
USA/Canada	00 1

Water

Unless clearly stated otherwise, tap water is safe to drink everywhere. The water on Madeira is fresh, sourced from pure mountain springs and of high quality.

The water on Porto Santo is desalinated, and is also quite safe to drink.

Bottled water is available everywhere, and it is important to drink lots of water daily to avoid dehydration. Still water is água sem gás, while água com gás is likely to be naturally sparkling.

Other Considerations
Family Fun?

There used to be a time when Madeira was considered an exclusive resort for middle-aged and elderly travellers, and that category of visitor rightly still finds the island endlessly fascinating and relaxing. But increasingly, Madeira is proving to be a successful and enjoyable family destination, too. The absence of golden sandy beaches is not a problem – in fact some children find it amusing to be playing in black sand – and is compensated for by extensive provision for children at virtually every major hotel across the island, from paddling pools and shallow swimming pools to play areas and theme parks like the Aqua Parque at Santa

Cruz. There are numerous attractions and trips, from a half-day out in the Bay on a replica of Christopher Columbus's ship looking for dolphins and whales to helicopter flights over the island.

Nor should eating out be a problem; the Madeiran restaurants love to see children day or night.

Women Travellers

Madeira is generally regarded as a very safe place for unescorted women, where they will be treated with good old-fashioned respect. With a modicum of common sense, it is perfectly safe for a woman to walk alone, and can often do so without the wake of wolf whistles that are heard in other European destinations.

In general, Madeiran women dress conservatively; shorts and scanty tops mark you as a tourist, but are not likely to cause offence, except perhaps in churches.

Topless sunbathing for a long time was largely unknown other than around a few hotel swimming pools, but there is a slight increase in 'toplessness' (but not total nudity) on some of the more secluded beaches. It is still very much the norm around hotel pools, and is unlikely to cause either offence or interest.

The Gay Scene

Madeiran people tend to be rather conservative in their outlook, so there is no open support for gay or lesbian couples, and no 'gay scene' as such. But neither is there any marked resentment. Many of the hotels know that gay or lesbian people stay with them and are more than happy for them to do so. And it is increasingly obvious that low-profile gay people are finding Madeira a pleasant and agreeable destination.

Driving

Driving on Madeira is fun, but it is also demanding. Porto Santo is much less complicated.

You drive on the right, as in most European countries, and there is a good degree of uniformity with other European road signs and directions, sufficient at least for a ready understanding of them. But for anyone intent on hiring a car – and there is much to be said for it – there are a few things to bear in mind about Madeira.

Above: *The familiar yellow Mercedes taxis wait along the Avenida Arriaga in Funchal. Taxis offer an inexpensive way of getting around, and can be hired for a whole day.*

Firstly, with the exception of Funchal, few roads are straight, and even fewer on the level. Away from the coast, the mountain roads are serpentine at best, at worst scary. This is not conducive to high speeds, and a lot of time will be spent changing gear – for this reason alone it is a good idea if hiring a car to opt for one with a powerful engine rather than thinking that a smaller engine will give better fuel consumption. Quite a few hill road require first gear in a small car.

Secondly, although they are improving, away from Funchal, the roads are generally in poor condition, which is not surprising when you consider that gravity is permanently trying to push them all down to the sea. So, expect extended areas of uneven surface with cracks, sloping verges, potholes, raised or sunken manhole covers and a poor state of repair. And take care on enter-

ing inland tunnels; the road surface can change rather quickly inside the tunnel because of water action.

In Madeira it is mandatory for drivers and passengers to wear seat belts.

Keep an eye open for any road sign that is square, blue, and has a number (usually 40, 60 or 80) in it; this is a warning sign to let you know that you are approaching some particular hazard – a difficult entry point to the expressway, a long descent, or a bad junction, for example. Speed limits in blue squares are advisory, those in blue circles are compulsory.

The 'Expressways'

There are only two 'high speed' roads: the ViaLitoral (via rapida), from Machico to Ribeira Brava, and the ViaExpresso, which runs from Santana south towards, but not quite reaching, Machico.

The upper speed limit is 100kph (62 mph) (but it is variable), and there are proposals to try to reduce this.

On both expressways, it is obligatory to use dipped

headlights at all times. Exits are well signed, but joining slip roads are short, with the result that you may often find a queue of cars waiting to join, and then quite frequently doing so at slow speed.

Because the expressways make travel across the island so much easier, they are (ironically) well used by slow-moving lorries that often cause equally slow-moving bottlenecks. Beware of the possibility of encountering lorries when you enter any of the many tunnels.

Town and Inland Driving

Away from the expressways, there are still many tunnels to negotiate; it is obligatory to use dipped headlights in tunnels. The speed limit on principal roads is 80kph (50mph), and on urban roads either 60kph (37mph) or 40kph (25mph).

At road junctions 'STOP' means stop, not creep forward. Unlike in some European countries, flashing headlights do not mean an oncoming driver is giving way – quite the contrary, he's coming through. Flashing headlights should be treated only as a warning, nothing else.

Parking

Finding somewhere to park at street level in Funchal is difficult, and metered (except on Sundays and public holidays). But there are a number of underground car parks where rates are very cheap. Increasingly, underground parking areas are developing in other main centres. But beware: if you are not accustomed to driving a left-hand drive vehicle the underground car parks can feel a little restricted, and many a wing mirror has met many a wall.

Meters on outdoor car parks are not in operation on Sundays, but don't be surprised in rural areas to be approached by a local lad asking for money to 'look after' your car. It's up to you whether you give him 1 or 2€, and there is absolutely no guarantee that it will make a scrap of difference, but at least you will have made someone who probably needs it a few euros happier!

Fuel

Petrol (gasoline) is lead free (sem chumbo) at octanes 95 and 98; diesel (gasóleo) is also widely available.

Most towns and villages have petrol stations, usually open 08:00 until 20:00, and most take credit cards. Some petrol stations in Funchal are open 24/7.

Breakdowns

There is no central breakdown and rescue service on Madeira because all visitors use hire cars. So, the hire car companies run their own breakdown service, and on hiring a car you will be given documentation with the number to call in an emergency. Remember to leave these documents in the glove compartment of the car; you may also need them if stopped by the police.

If you happen to break down on the expressways, there is Assistência, a recovery service that will get you onto neighbouring roads. The principal aim of Assistência is to keep the expressway clear, but you will find that its operators will help you to resolve your difficulties.

There are two numbers to ring 800 290 290 for the ViaLitoral around Funchal, and 800 20 30 40 for the ViaExpresso between Santana and Machico.

Car Rental

Having your own car is the most flexible way of getting around Madeira, and is well worth considering. Given the size of Madeira, nowhere is beyond a day trip by car, although trying to get around the whole coast road in a day, while possible, is a rather daunting proposition, and not to be entertained.

There are both major and local car rental companies on Madeira, offering competitive rates. You can usually book your car in advance through a travel agent, through your hotel, online or on arrival at the airport.

If you plan on using a car for the greater part of your stay, it is better to arrange to collect and return the car to the Funchal airport. The car rental desks are in the 'Arrivals' hall. At Santa Catarina (Funchal) airport, car rental is available from:

- Avis, tel: (+351) 291 523 392
- Auto Jardim, tel: (+351) 291 524 023
- Drive Car Rental, tel: (+351) 291 523 355
- Europcar, tel: (+351) 291 524 633
- Hertz, tel: (+351) 291 523 040
- Rodavante, tel: (+351) 291 524 718

Car rental is available at Porto Santo airport from:

- Auto Jardim, tel: (+351) 291 984 937
- Rodavante, tel: (+351) 291 982 925
- Moinho Rent-a-Car, tel: (+351) 291 982 780

Don't forget your driving licence.

Taxis

Both on Madeira and Porto Santo, the ubiquitous yellow taxis (mostly Mercedes) are relatively inexpensive, and trips usually metered, although there are fixed charges (set annually) for certain trips such as from the airport. There are surcharges for extra luggage and for travel between 22:00 and 07:00, or on Sundays and public holidays.

If an approaching taxi is showing a green light on its roof, you can flag it down, especially in rural areas.

There are a number of taxi ranks in Funchal, but a long section of the Avenida Arriaga is being pedestrianized (2006) and this may affect what has long been one of the main taxi ranks in the town. The main taxi rank on Porto Santo is in Cidade Vila Baleira on Rua Dr Nuno Silvestre Teixeira.

In the highly unlikely event that you have a disagreeable experience with the manner or behaviour of a taxi driver, don't argue, just note the number on the side of the car, and report the incident to the tourist office. Procedures exist to deal with unacceptable behaviour on the part of licensed taxi drivers.

Book a taxi for a tour

One excellent way of getting around is to book a taxi for a half or full day. Ask at your hotel if they know taxi drivers with a good command of English or your own language, and then negotiate a rate. Moreover, you get a good deal of information this way, much of it enjoyable, gossipy, chatty, friendly and entertaining. You also get to control where you go.

Bus Travel

Changes to bus timetables are quite frequent. If you intend making use of buses then for a small cost you can get 'Madeira by Bus' at tourist offices. Be sure to arrive in good time at bus stations; the buses leave on time, and it may take you a while to find the right one!

Madeira: Madeira has an excellent bus transport network serving almost every part of the island, and it can be quite an enlightening experience in itself to take a trip by bus. But the bus service is geared to the needs of local people, and this can make day trips difficult. Bus stops are marked 'Paragem', and usually have timetables. Buses are generally modern, clean (within the constraints of the service) and comfortable, and have a good safety record.

In and around Funchal, buses are operated by Horários do Funchal (Tel: 291 705 555). The north and west of the island is served by Rodoeste (Tel: 291 233 830), with buses departing from Rua Ribeira João Gomes in Funchal. SAM buses (Tel: 291 706 710) operate in the east and northeast of the island, including the airport, and depart from Rua Calouste Gulbenkian, Funchal. A number of smaller companies, with departures from the Old Town end of Avenida do Mar in Funchal, cover the rest of the island: Companhia dos Carros de São Gonçalo (to Camacha, Santo da Serra, the north and Curral das Freiras); Empresa de Automóveis do Caniço (to Caniço); and São Roque do Faial (to the north coast via Ribeira Frio).

In Funchal, the main bus stops, and ticket kiosks, are on Avenida do Mar (the seafront). Cancel your ticket as you board the bus. Seven-day passes, valid on all routes, are available to visitors.

Porto Santo: Horários de Transportes operate six bus routes around Porto Santo, but they are very much intended to meet the needs of local people, which means that you may have to wait a while for return buses.

Maps

Visitors accustomed to the British Ordnance Survey maps, or the French IGN maps will be amazed to find that there are no wholly reliable maps to Madeira and Porto Santo. So much is changing so quickly that it is impossible for mapmakers to keep pace with developments; there is no indexed street map of Funchal, for example. Things are not helped by poor road signing, especially away from Funchal, and, for that matter, even in the suburbs of Funchal. If you do buy a map, check to see that it is a fairly recent edition.

Newspapers and Magazines

Most main European newspapers are available at newsagents in Funchal the day after publication. There are also a number of free English-language newspapers, like The Madeira Times, which provides up-to-date information, some advertising and a few interesting articles that provide background information.

2006 saw the introduction of a splendid English-language quarterly magazine 'Essential Madeira and Porto Santo'. It's crammed with information, lots of glossy ads and well-written contributions on everything from golf to cuisine, fashion to festivals. Look out for it at the news kiosks in Funchal. Some of the better hotels provide it in their rooms.

Public Toilets

Most public toilets in Funchal have a resident attendant who expects (in some cases, demands) a small tip in return for the cleanliness of his/her realm. You tip according to what you find. Outside Funchal, the public toilets are not brilliant, and a better bet is to call in a café for a coffee and use their toilets.

Cavalheiros, Homens and Senhores all mean 'Gents'; 'Ladies' is Senhoras.

Language

Even Madeirans are inclined to admit that Portuguese is a difficult language to master. But most Madeirans speak excellent English, taught at school, along with French and German.

There are two distinctive Portuguese sounds that can be confusing at first. Nasal vowels, written with a til (~), produce an unusual sound – 'bread', pão is pronounced 'Pow!', with a strong nasal ring. 'S' and 'Z' are often softened to a slushy 'sh' sound. So, 'tourism', tourismo is pronounced 'too-rish-mo'.

Below: A modern form of azujelo tiling, which is found opposite the Monte cable car entrance, promotes the spectacular Monte Palace Gardens. The old palace itself is not open to the public, but the gardens are an excellent reason for using the cable car to reach this hilltop village.

Contact Details
Hotels
Quinta Jardins do Lago
(see page 104)
Rua Dr João Lemos Gomes 29
São Pedro,
9000-208 Funchal
tel: (+351) 291 750 100
fax: (+351) 291 750 150
info@jardins-lago.pt
www.jardins-lago.com

Hotel Royal Savoy (see page 104)
Avenida do Infante
9004 542 Funchal
tel: (+351) 291 213 000
tax: (+351) 291 223 103
savoyreservation@netmadeira.com
www.savoyresort.com

Quinta Bela de São Tiago
(see page 106)
Rua Bela de São Tiago, 70
9060-400 Funchal
tel: (+351) 291 204 500
fax: (+351) 291 204 510
hotel.qta.bela.s.tiago@
mail.telepac.pt
www.hotel-qta-bela-s-tiago.com

Quinta Bela Vista (see page 109)
Caminho do Avista Navios 4
9000-129 Funchal
tel: (+351) 291 706 400
fax: (+351) 291 706 401
qbvista@netmadeira.com
www.qbvista.pt

Quinta Perestrello (see page 109)
Rua do Dr Pita 3
9000-089 Funchal
tel: (+351) 291 706 700
fax: (+351) 291 706 706
quintaperestrelo@
charminghotelsmadeira.com
www.charminghotelsmadeira.com

Quinta do Monte (see page 110)
Caminho do Monte, 1922
9050-288 Funchal
tel: (+351) 291 780 100
fax: (+351) 291 780 110
quintamonte@charminghotels
madeira.com
www.charminghotelsmadeira.com

Quinta Estreito (see page 111)
Rua José Joaquim da Costa 9325-
034 Estreito da Câmara de Lobos

tel: (+351) 291 910 530
fax: (+351) 291 910 549
quintaestreito@charminghotels
madeira.com
www.charminghotelsmadeira.com

Hotel Calheta Beach
(see page 112)
P-9370-133 Calheta
tel: (+351) 291 820 300
fax: (+351) 291 820 301
calheta-beach@galoresort.com
www.galoresort.com

Átrio (see page 112–113)
Lombo dos Moinhos Acima
9370-217 Estreito da Calheta
tel: (+351) 291 820 400
fax: (+351) 291 820 419
welcome@atrio-madeira.com
www.atrio-madeira.com

Hotel Moniz Sol (see page 113)
Vila do Porto Moniz
9270-095 Porto moniz
tel: (+351) 291 850 150
fax: (+351) 291 850 155
informa@hotelmonizsol.com
www.hotelmonizsol.com

Estalagem do Mar (*see* page 116)
Juncos, Fajã da Areia
9240 São Vicente
tel: (+351) 291 840 010
fax: (+351) 291 840 019
estalagem.mar@mail.telepac.pt
www.estalagemdomar.com

Hotel O Colmo (*see* page 116)
Sítio do Serrado
9230-116 Santana
tel: (+351) 291 570 290
fax: (+351) 291 574 312
info@hotelocolmo.com
www.hotelocolmo.com

Hotel Quinta Splendida
(*see* page 117)
Estrada da Ponta da Oliviera, 11
9125-001 Caniço
tel: (+351) 291 930 400
fax: (+351) 291 930 401
info@quintasplendida.com
www.quintasplendida.com

Quinta Serra Golfe (*see* page 119)
Casais Próximos, Santo da Serra
9100-255 Santa Cruz
tel: (+351) 291 550 500

estalagem@serragolf.com
www.serragolf.com

Estalagem Eira do Serrado
(*see* page 119)
Curral das Freiras
tel: (+351) 291 710 060
fax: (+351) 291 710 061
eiradoserrado@mail.telepac.pt
www.eiradoserrado.com

Hotel Porto Santo (*see* page 119)
Riberio Cochino
Campo do Baixo, Porto Santo
tel: (+351) 291 980 140
www.hotelportosanto.com

Restaurants
Xôpana
Travessa do Largo da Coupana
tel: (+351) 291 206 020

O Casa Velha
Palheiro Golf
tel: (+351) 291 790 350

O Barqueiro
Rua Ponta da Cruz, Funchal
tel: (+351) 291 761 229

Casa Mãe, Quinta Bela Vista
(*see* page 150)
Reservations: tel: (+351) 291 706 400

Mar Azul
tel: (+351) 291 230 079

Marina Terrace
tel: (+351) 291 230 547.

Beer House
tel: (+351) 291 229 011

Fu Hao
Marina Shopping Centre, Avenida Arriaga
tel: (+351) 291 281 099

Casa Portuguesa
Travessa das Torres, 30, Old Town
tel: (+351) 291 228 446

Gavião Novo
Rua de Santa Maria, 131, Old Town, tel: (+351) 291 229 238

Below: All the luxury of the indoor spa at the Royal Savoy Hotel.

**Bacchus Restaurant, Hotel
Quinta Estreito** (*see* page 111)
Reservations: tel: (+351) 291 910
530

Adega da Quinta
Reservations: tel: (+351) 291 910
530

Casa da Vinha
Rue dos Lavradores 4, Sitio de Pico
e Saloes, 9325 Estreito da Câmara
de Lobos. Reservations (recommended): tel: (+315) 962 816 705.

Restaurant Eucalipto
tel: (+351) 291 951 282.

La Perla, Hotel Quinta Splendida
(*see* page 117)
Reservations: tel: (+351) 291 930
400

Restaurant O Colmo
tel: (+351) 291 570 290

O Calhetas
tel: (+351) 291 984 380

Sport
Diving
Manta Diving Center
Galo Resort Hotels, Galomar, Rua
Robert Baden Powell, 9125 036
Caniço de Baixo
tel/fax: (+351) 291 935 588
stefan@mantadiving.com
www.mantadiving.com

Tubarão Madeira Mergulho Lda.
Hotel Pestana Palms, Rua do Vale
das Neves 73, 9050 332 Funchal
tel: (+351) 291 709 227

tubarao.madeira@netmadeira.com
www.scuba-madeira.com

Porto Santo Sub
tel: (+351) 291 983 259
portosantosub@sapo.pt
www.portosantosub.com

Boat Trips and Sea Watching
Ventura do Mar
Marina do Funchal, Pontão B.
tel: (+351) 291 280 033
venturadomar@iol.pt
www.venturadomar.com

Yacht Gavião
tel: (+351) 291 241 124
gaviaomadeira@netmadeira.com

Sea Pleasure Catamaran
tel: (+351) 291 224 900
info@madeiracatamaran.com
www.madeiracatamaran.com

Sea Born Catamaran
tel: (+351) 291 231 312
seaborn@netmadeira.com
www.catamaran-seaborn.com

Deep-sea Fishing
Albatroz do Mar
Marina do Funchal, 9000-055
Funchal
tel: (+351) 96 300 3864
albatrozdomar@sapo.pt

Fish Madeira
Travessa das Virtudes, 123, 9000-
664 Funchal, tel: (+351) 291 752
685 or (+351) 91 759 9990
bristow@netmadeira.com
www.fishmadeira.com

Livremar – Freed´em
tel: (+351) 291 934 996 or (+351)
96 320 9717
info@madeirabiggame.com
www.biggamecharters.com

Madeira Big Game Fishing
tel: (+351) 291 231 823 or (+351)
96 612 4750
madeirafishing@mail.telepac.pt
www.madeiragamefish.com

Nautisantos Big Game Fishing
Rua Dr. António Jardim de
Oliveira, 2, 9050-171 Funchal
tel: (+351) 291 231 312 or
(+351) 91 991 6221
enquiries@nautisantosfishing.com
www.nautisantosfishing.com

Xiphias Sport Fishing Charters
Marina do Funchal
9000 Funchal
tel: (+351) 291 280 007 or (+351)
91 928 8970
xiphias_charters@yahoo.com
http://xiphias.no.sapo.pt

Football
Maritimo
Barreiros Stadium
Rua do Dr Pita
Funchal
Club shop
Rua Dom Carlos 14, Funchal
www.maritimomadeira.com

Nacional
Estádio E Rui Alves
Choupana
Club shop
Rua do Esmeraldo, Funchal
www.nacional-da-madeira.com

Helpful Words and Phrases

English	Portuguese
Basics	
Yes	Sim
No	Não
Please	Se faz favour/Por favor
Thank you	Obrigado/obrigada
Hello	Olá
Goodbye	Adeus
Good morning	Bom dia
Good evening/good night	Bom noite
Sorry/pardon	Perdão
Do you speak English?	Fala ingles
Left	À esquerda
Right	À direita
Straight ahead	Sempre em frente

Places	
Airport	Aeroporto
Bus station	Estação de camionetas
Bus	Autocarro
Bus stop	Paragem
Hospital	Hospital
Hotel	Hotel/estalagem
Market	Mercado
Museum	Museu
Street	Rua
Taxi rank	Praça de taxis

Numbers	
1	Um (una)
2	Dois (duas)
3	Três
4	Quarto
5	Cinco
6	Seis
7	Sete
8	Oito
9	Nove
10	Dez
11	Onze
12	Doze
13	Treze
14	Catorze
15	Quinze
16	Dezasseis
17	Dezassete
18	Dezoito
19	Deznove
20	Vinte
21	Vinte e um
30	Trinta
40	Quarenta
50	Cinquenta
60	Sessenta
70	Setenta
80	Oitenta
90	Noventa
100	Cemi/cento
1000	Mil

Days	
Monday	Segunda-feira
Tuesday	Terça-feira
Wednesday	Quarta-feira
Thursday	Quinta-feira
Friday	Sexta-feira
Saturday	Sábado
Sunday	Domingo

Food/restaurants	
Menu	Ementa
Mineral water	Água
(with/without gas)	(com/sem gás)
Tea	Chá
Coffee	Café
With/without milk	Com/sem leite
Sugar	Açúcar
The bill	A conta

First edition published in 2007
by New Holland Publishers (UK) Ltd
London • Cape Town • Sydney • Auckland

10 9 8 7 6 5 4 3 2 1

website: www.newhollandpublishers.com

Garfield House, 86 Edgware Road
London W2 2EA
United Kingdom

80 McKenzie Street
Cape Town 8001
South Africa

14 Aquatic Drive
Frenchs Forest, NSW 2086
Australia

218 Lake Road
Northcote, Auckland
New Zealand

Distributed in the USA by
The Globe Pequot Press
Connecticut

ISBN 978 1 84537 555 3

Although every effort has been made to ensure that this guide
is up to date and current at time of going to print, the
Publisher accepts no responsibility or liability for any loss,
injury or inconvenience incurred by readers or travellers using
this guide.

Publishing Manager: Thea Grobbelaar
DTP Cartographic Manager: Genené Hart
Editor: Thea Grobbelaar
Design and DTP: Nicole Bannister
Cartographer: Nicole Bannister
Picture Research: Shavonne Govender
Proofreader: Carla Zietsman
Indexer: Carla Zietsman
Reproduction by Resolution, Cape Town
Printed and bound in China by C & C Offset Printing Co., Ltd.

Photographic Credits:
jonarnoldimages.com/Walter Bibikow: page 68; **jonanold
images.com/Rex Butcher:** page 74; **DRTM (Direcção Regional
de Turismo Madeira):** half title page, contents page, pages 8–9,
12, 16–17, 28, 60–61, 82, 90, 92–93, 94–95, 126, 128, 143, 144,
156–157, 158, 160, 161, 162–163, 164, 165, 166; **Hotel Porto
Santo:** page 59; **International Photobank:** page 79; **International Photobank/Adrian Baker:** pages 30–31, 38;
International Photobank/Jeanetta Baker: page 53;
International Photobank/Peter Baker: cover, page 155; **Terry
Marsh:** pages 15, 19, 27, 32, 33, 35, 37, 40, 41, 44, 45, 46–47,
49, 50–51, 54, 64–65, 66, 67, 75, 76, 77, 78, 86–87, 89, 109,
110–111, 112, 113, 117, 118, 119, 120–121, 125, 130–131, 133,
134–135, 138, 151, 168–169, 170, 174, 180, 182, 185; **Paul
Murphy:** page 84; **Photo Access:** page 145; **Pictures Colour
Library:** pages 22, 42, 57, 62, 72–73, 122, 132, 139, 172–173;
Quinta Bela São Tiago: pages 96–97, 106–107; **Quinta da Bela
Vista:** pages 6, 20, 80, 108, 136, 140, 146, 148–149; **Quinta
Jardins do Lago:** pages 10, 100, 102–103; **Quinta Splendida:**
title page, pages 24–25, 114–115, 152–153; **Royal Savoy:** pages
98, 105, 186–187; **Travel-Images.com:** page 71.

Keep us Current
Information in travel guides is apt to change, which is why
we regularly update our guides. We'd be grateful to receive
feedback if you've noted something we should include in our
updates. If you have new information, please share it with us
by writing to the Publishing Manager, Globetrotter, at the
office nearest to you (addresses on this page). The most
significant contribution to each new edition will receive a
free copy of the updated guide.

Cover: *View of Ponta do Sol.*
Half title: *Funchal Marina.*
Title page: *View of Funchal from Quinta Splendida.*
Contents page: *The golden beach of Porto Santo island.*